SPACE
CARROTS!

A NOVEL

SPACE CARROTS!

JOSH CARROTT

Compass-Publishing UK

Space Carrots! © Josh Carrott & Ollie Kendal

Compass-Publishing UK 2023

ISBN 978-1-915962-31-7

Ghost-written by Ollie Kendal

Ghost-ghost-written by Jenny Lee and Andy Brierley

Cover artwork © Ben Thomas 2023
Illustrations © Ben Thomas 2023
Song *The Prophecy in Carrotland* by Andy Kyte, Ollie Kendal,
Jenny Lee and Andy Brierley

For Lizzie and Gabie

Contents

About the Author

Joshua Daryl Carrott was born in 1988 and raised in Caterham, Southern England, and then Qingdao, Eastern China. It was at international school in Qingdao that he developed a love for Korea, having been befriended by fellow Korean students. He is married to Gabie Kook, and they live in London with their adorable dog, Brie. Josh spends most of his time making silly videos with his best friend, Ollie Kendal.

In 2021 Josh became the first person in history to unknowingly write and publish his own autobiography, Once Upon a Time in Carrotland, which went on to become a global bestseller. His voice was later synthesised using artificial intelligence to produce an audiobook of the aforementioned autobiography, making him the first person to unknowingly read and record his own audiobook. The funds from these endeavours were used to build a carrot rocket statue in Carrotland, New Zealand which was unveiled on April 1st, 2023. He finds all of this hilarious.

1

An Unveiling

It was a perfect day in Carrotland. The birds were shining, the sun was singing, the wind was falling on the ground in large splashes, and the trees were doing whatever it is trees do all day while the rest of us are working. Probably worrying about weak-bladdered dogs. The clean mountain air was thick with the aroma of carrot blossom, and the vegetable themed adventure park was alive with the electric thrum of anticipation. The day was April 1st 2023, the time was late-morning, and although it was only 170 years to the day since Cincinnati became the first US city to employ full time professional firefighters, none of the people gathered on that fateful day were thinking about that. They were thinking about destiny.

Personally, I have always thought that tales of destiny are the deluded nonsense of a fanciful brain. While some people may find comfort in the belief that their lives are guided by fate, the truth is that predestination is codswallop and kismet is hogwash. Believing in such pig-swill can be limiting and discouraging, as it takes away our agency and the power to make our own decisions. Believe me, I've tried it, and it was rubbish. Unlike in fairytale love stories, which I wholeheartedly believe in, destiny has never made my stomach leap anywhere, and no fireworks of emotion have ever exploded over the landscape of my life as the result of a particularly big dollop of fate. But putting all that to one side, this day did seem pretty darned momentous.

As the clock on the town hall struck 11:42 the crowd grew restless, eagerly awaiting the big moment. Suddenly a cry went out and all eyes turned towards a small but very clean tractor turning off the Volcanic Loop highway into the car park. The tractor slowed then stopped, as they often do, and out jumped an extremely handsome YouTuber, grinning from ear to ear in an orange Nasa jumpsuit which really suited him. (It was me - Josh Carrott, Caterham Golf Club's most promising under-7 newcomer 1993). As I stepped up to the stage for the introductory speeches, I was met with the most incredible sight I've ever seen. It wasn't just the tens of people we'd expected, this was easily tens of tens. Tens of fifteens, even. Possibly even hundreds of fives. My brain, struggling to process the sight before me, went into flashback mode, to remind me of some important context in case I was new to all this.

I had first stumbled upon Carrotland in 2017, whilst on an epic road trip across New Zealand with Gabie my wife, Ollie my first wife, and Lizzie, Ollie's first wife. Our friends Sho and Andy were there too, but I'm not married to either of them (yet). After a wonderful week meandering around north North Island, we were heading south towards south North Island, before crossing the Cook Strait to north South Island. Still with me? We had paused en route from Auckland to Wellington to climb Mount Doom from the Harry Potter movies, when we saw to our right a seven metre tall colossus, an orange spectacle so wondrous that it's difficult to describe, but I'll try. It was the world's largest carrot, made of wood and fibreglass. Oh, actually that wasn't too difficult.

Spellbound, we dismounted from our carriages (I always travel by carriage due to a life-long fear of speed), and filmed what would go on to become one of the greatest YouTube videos in the whole world, nay, universe, nay, galaxy! Entitled THE WORLD'S BIGGEST CARROT?! it was an action-packed 7-minute thrill ride through all the vegetable-themed enticements the park had to offer. We released it to a waiting world in May 2017, and it's fair to say it struck a chord so quiet that it was audible only to dogs. But while it may not have inspired many viewers, it sure inspired me. The source of my inspiration was in fact not the video, but a peculiar prophecy I'd received from my imaginary carrot best friend, Muncho, who'd been my erstwhile companion since my third birthday. The prophecy, delivered in unison by a pyramid of anthropomorphic carrots that no-one else had seen, foretold a book as yet unwritten and a mighty statue around which I would discover my destiny. As a great believer in destiny, this ticked all my boxes, jangled all my jingles, and hit all the keys on my accordion of joy.

With each passing year, on the anniversary of this momentous episode, my colossally talented and refreshingly humble co-host Ollie made sure we filmed some sort of carrot-themed celebration, each one more magnificent and pointless than the last. In the words of the great poet and chef Andrea Zagatti, it was a crescendo which did not descendo, which technically meant that it couldn't have a peak. But if it had, it would surely have been the moment in 2021 when Ollie, in genius mode as usual, wrote and published the completely accurate and entertaining autobiography of my life without my knowledge. What a guy!

He was unaware of course, because he'd been in the toilet at the time of the prophecy, that he had just fulfilled one of its key tenets: a bestselling book! He could never have known, I know. But as I always say, "when you know, you know. You know?" But not only did he not know, he didn't even know that he didn't know. Oh no.

The book went on to sell over 15,000 copies, and the proceeds had funded the park's second carroty behemoth, which now stood before me in 2023. Unlike the original giant carrot, which towered proudly over the park's entrance like a salady sentinel, our statue marked a real turning point in vegetable statue design. It was in the shape of a rocket, with beautiful green leafy boosters and a control panel in case of the unlikely event that it needed to be flown to another planet (well you never know, you know?). It was the most beautiful thing I'd ever seen apart from Gabie, and it made me swell with pride to know that our fans, the Jollybeans, and Ollie's genius had made this happen.

As I surveyed the crowd and absorbed the enormity of what was happening, I was bemused and honoured, bemonoured if you will, and completely speechless, which was really unfortunate because at that very moment I was called up to deliver a speech to the massive crowd of over 5,000 people. I was dizzy with nerves. I closed one of my eyes to help me calm down, and when I opened it and gazed upon the 10,000 people before me, I felt like I was seeing double.

Looking out at the crowd, many of whom were wearing the special limited edition "Visit Carrotland" t-shirts that Ollie had designed in a fit of characteristic creative brilliance, I began to speak.

"Wow." I said, poetically. "Golly gosh."

The crowd cheered.

"Crikey" I said, and I meant it.

Luckily for posterity and the people present, at this point I remembered that Ollie (who couldn't be there due to a back injury) had supplied me with the speech he'd planned to give, and asked me to deliver it on his behalf. I gathered myself, took in a deep breath, and intoned the words that would echo through the ages:

> *Ladies and gentlemen, boys and girls, Jollybeans, Carrotnauts and local dignitaries.*
>
> *At an auspicious time such as this, it seems entirely appropriate to quote President Kennedy. (I won't do the accent, though.)*
>
> *We choose to go to the moon. Not because it is easy, but because it is hard, because that goal will serve to organise and measure the best of our energies and skills, because that challenge is one that we are willing to accept, one we are unwilling to postpone, and one which we intend to win.*
>
> *Some might say that President Kennedy probably wasn't talking about our rocket, because it was only built a month ago and he died in 1963.*

They might go on to say that there is little similarity between mankind's most astounding achievement and the construction of a fibreglass rocket in a rural town in Ruapehu.

These people are, of course, idiots. Just as the Apollo rockets represented the pinnacle of technology and engineering, the magnificent craft beside me shows just what is possible when you have a dream, a best-selling autobiography which you know nothing about, and the force of nature that is Carrotland co-founder Dave Scott.

Like the moon landings, many people doubted that this would ever happen. For a long time it looked like the Soviet Union would win the vegetable space race with their potato based satellite Spudnik, but I stand before you today, a triumphant and proud Carrot.

This rocket represents the triumph of determination over necessity, of form over function, and of dreams over reality.

It is not often in life that one gets to be part of something as ridiculous but wonderful as this, and I am humbled to stand before you now in this fetching orange jumpsuit and officially launch this carrot into the cosmos.

So without further ado, let's get this baby airborne! Kabooya!

The crowd went wild, partly because that's what crowds do, but mainly because my speech was so amazingly perfect for the occasion. Those gathered couldn't have known that I'd actually given it verbatim at my wedding to Gabie, but somehow it seemed even more appropriate here.

With the festivities winding to a close and the crowd of at least 20,000 people slowly dispersing into the queue for the free-to-use Portaloos, I felt a sense of gratitude and humility wash over me. Grumility, if you will. Actually, maybe it was closer to wonder and awe. Wawe, perhaps? Or awnder? I don't feel confident about that one, but the point is I was pretty darned astoundazed.

SPACE CARROTS! – A Novel

It was mind-boggling to think that I, the world's greatest but most humble carrot, was about to join the pantheon of galactic greats: Yuri Gagarin, Lance Armstrong, Buzz Lightyear, Lando Calrissian, and Jeff Bezos.

But now, with the prophecy fulfilled, it was time to go home. I missed my second wife Gabie and my furball friend Brie. As we walked past the Portaloos, we began to say our goodbyes to the carroty contingent. I mentioned to Muncho how excited I was to get home and reunite with my loved ones. I thought he would be pleased for me about all the love in my life, but instead he was outraged.

"What about the prophecy?!" he yelled. Luckily carrots can't yell that loud, so it didn't throw me too far emotionally out of whack, but I was concerned.

"What about the prophecy?" I asked, around 50% agog.

"Don't you remember it?" Muncho cried. He was clearly pretty stressed out.

"Of course I do," I snapped. It may have been six years ago, but I could hardly forget it. "It blew my mind. I couldn't move my neck for a week. But we've written the book. We've built the statue. The prophecy is fulfilled. I feel a great sense of calm and completion. Don't you?"

"No I do not, Joshua Daryl Carrott! Listen to it again and this time turn your brain on!"

Kindly, Muncho reminded me of the prophecy in its entirety from beginning to end, in case it had been a long time since I'd read the first book.

> *"Joshua Daryl Carrott,*
> *our master, friend and root,*
> *Thank goodness Ollie brought you here,*
> *his brain is most astute.*
> *So hear the carrot prophecy,*
> *a-calling from afar,*

> *to you adorned with extra "t",*
> *our orange YouTube tsar!*
> *A book as yet unwritten,*
> *your story bold and true,*
> *shelves stacked and readers smitten,*
> *chart topping, plus a few.*
> *And as the sales grow bigger,*
> *they'll raise a timely sum,*
> *to build this park a figure,*
> *for you, our carrot son.*
> *For this the place, but not the time,*
> *to reveal with great fanfare,*
> *a mighty statue most sublime,*
> *and meet your purpose there."*

I wondered for a few seconds about the power of poetry, when Muncho demanded,

"Do you feel like you've met your purpose? Have you had a new revelation about your destiny? Hmm?!"

I tried to explain my theory about destiny, fate, and the deluded nonsense of fanciful brains, but he was having none of it. Something in me suspected he was right, but I didn't want to believe it, and we got into a heated battle of wits. Both of us knew that there was something special about this place and that the prophecy meant more than just small talk, even if I only knew it very deep down in the dusty basement of my brain. But I just couldn't understand why this meant we needed to stay. Life had to go on. The statue was built. This chapter was nearly over.

I'm ashamed to say that at points my emotions got the better of me and I said some things that were just plain mean.

"All this talk of the prophecy is ridiculous!" I shouted, losing my head completely. "We've done everything it says, but you're still not satisfied. Sometimes I think you'd be more useful julienned and chucked in a casserole with lots of lentils!"

There was a long silence, a pregnant pause, a moment suffused with a foreshadowing tension, like a planet core about to blow. It was Muncho's turn to be agog.

"Lentils?!" he asked, visibly shaken. Then suddenly enraged, "Are you even aware of how gassy lentils make you? And you're about to get on a flight, you idiot!"

"You're the idiot!" I retorted, cleverly.

"No, you are!" Muncho screamed back.

I paused, dramatically, unsure how to respond to this level of repartee. Then I bent down to stare Muncho straight in the face, and whispered calmly, "You're the biggest idiot in the whole wide world. No returns."

That foxed him. Zinger delivered, I stood up and walked angrily away from Muncho and the rocket, towards the original giant carrot at the entrance to the park. In my fury I punched the enormous vegetable, which caused it to wobble and creak before settling at an alarming angle, like the leaning tower of Pisa, but made of carrots instead of peas. Muncho remained where I'd left him, standing alone amidst all the commotion – still believing in something he couldn't explain or understand. The statue unveiling had not brought the resolution he had longed for. He looked again at the gleaming rocket statue. It was glorious, but he couldn't believe it was the end of the story. The last line of the prophecy hung in the air between us, like a fart.

"...and meet your purpose there."

I had reached the road, and the carriage that was waiting to take me to the airport. I turned to look at my erstwhile carrot compadre. It really didn't look like he was budging. Destiny was something we'd always disagreed on, and I'd long ago accepted that it was our fate to do so, but he really needed to let things go sometimes. Unveiling a statue seemed purposeful enough for one day, and I was done with destiny. As I climbed into the waiting coach I heard the distant sound of Muncho starting to sing Happy Birthday to himself in a soft and soothing voice - a practice he has always resorted to in times of great stress.

Pulling away from the kerb, I looked up from the Jane Austen compendium I was reading and turned to see Muncho climb ruefully inside the rocket. He looked sad and alone, and I already knew I had gone too far by wishing him stewed. But something in my heart prevented me from going back to him. Maybe it was pride or sensibility, sense or prejudice, or perhaps it was the carriage driver Emma's persuasion that we crack on because the traffic was going to be bad around the wuthering heights of Northanger Abbey. Whatever it was, I resisted the urge to go back and apologise, and we trundled off towards the airport.

As I settled the reindeer for the flight home (I always fly by enchanted sleigh due to a life-long fear of tray tables), in my mind's ear I could hear the sound of Muncho's singing, echoing off the walls of the rocket and the bucolic pastures of Ohakune. I imagined him sitting in the orange craft amongst a pile of candy wrappers and dashed hopes. For the first time since my third birthday, Muncho and I were estranged and apart. And our estrartion didn't feel good.

2

LIFT OFF

Unfortunately the sleigh had a puncture, so we had to go by grotty-tray-tabled-plane, like peasants. I don't know if you've ever tried to settle a reindeer into an airline seat, but it's a squeeze, let me tell you. There were antlers everywhere. Throughout the flight I tried not to think about the events of the afternoon, of Muncho's sad little face looking so despondent with its permanently raised eyebrows and lack of ears, but even 42 episodes of The News did little to distract me. I was relieved, therefore, when I saw the twinkling lights of London through the smog, and the pilot told us to buckle up for landing. I don't know if you've ever tried to buckle a reindeer up for landing, but it's tricky, let me tell you. There were hooves everywhere. I heartily wished they hadn't been recently shod and that I had been wearing a safety helmet, neck brace and gum shield.

Departing the aircraft my mind was swimming with confusion, like a confused swimmer. Muncho had babbled on about fulfilling the prophecy, but to coin a phrase, I couldn't make heads or tails of it. I was looking forward to putting my feet up, getting my head down, and figuring out what was going on. But fate, and the limits of physical flexibility, had other ideas.

I cleared passport control, did half an hour of mindful colouring and hurried towards the baggage carousel to claim my belongings. I don't know if you've ever tried to collect a reindeer from a luggage belt, but it's a whole kettle of fish, let me tell you. There were sleigh bells everywhere.

After some time, I reached the arrivals hall and was met by my familiar genius broski Ollie, whose poor old back had prevented him from coming to Carrotland. I gave him a hug, a high five and a leaping chest bump, which floored him for about 45 minutes. Then I generously lectured him about the benefits of neck braces for another 45 minutes, which I could tell was hugely appreciated. Having wasted an hour and a half, and caused quite a scene, I was starting to gather up the saddles when my right eye caught sight of a news broadcast playing on a nearby TV. My left eye joined it, and both eyes widened as I took in the scene playing out before me.

BREAKING NEWS:

"A singing carrot has been seen climbing into an unnecessarily large statue of a carrot-shaped rocket in central New Zealand."

At this my mind was instantly blown, because until this moment no-one else had ever been able to see Muncho, my imaginary carrot pal! Without the benefit of the neck brace that I had just given to Ollie, the news floored me and I went down like a burning swan being hit by a train. Ollie then repeated back to me verbatim the 45 minute lecture I had just given him, which I suppose I deserved, and passed me back my neck brace.

"Ollie!" I gibbered. "It's Muncho on the news!" Ollie had heard of Muncho, having written my accurate and excellent autobiography, but unbelievably he had never truly believed in him until now, believe it or not.

I was boggled, but, trusting the very good (and available for commission) writers, I assumed this would be explained later in the story, perhaps in Chapter 4. I quickly re-donned my neck brace, and thank goodness I did, because the next bit of breaking news nearly blew my head right off!

"Unbelievably, some time later the statue's boosters, thought to be purely decorative, ignited and blasted the rocket into space!"

Ollie, now sans neck brace, hit the deck again. The news was reporting live from Carrotland, which appeared to be in a state of pandemonium as locals and authorities scrambled to make sense of what was happening, just as we were, but they were much more runny-about-y and less lie-y-on-the-floor-y. The report continued:

"According to eyewitnesses, the faint sound of a little voice singing Happy Birthday was heard, after which the carrot rocket, just yesterday unveiled by British YouTube sensation Josh Carrott, suddenly started to vibrate and emit smoke before taking off into the sky."

I looked at Ollie. He looked at me. We looked at each other, basically. Then we each looked at a reindeer and got no emotional reaction at all, which was understandable as reindeers only care about sleighs and bells, really. The news was cutting to vox pop interviews, which I, personally, always find so helpful and illuminating when trying to understand what the blazes is going on. The newsreader, as usual, was displaying the perfect amount of emotional concern without sensationalising reality as she expertly elicited reactions from local people.

"Mrs. Ardern, you, a poor innocent former prime minister, were standing shockingly near this dangerous rocket when it recklessly went off, and presumably you avoided being mangled by mere inches. How terrified are you, on a scale of one to speechless with terror? Don't hold back please."

"I couldn't believe it! My kid was playing right next to that rocket, and I thought it was just a statue. It's all the more surprising given that, until very recently, I was in charge of all of New Zealand's top secret space projects and I've never heard anything about this! I'm just glad no one was hurt."

"Cripes," I said to Ollie, who was blinking the words "by jingo!" to me in Morse Code. Another former prime minister was now appearing on the screen.

"Mr. English, you were simply a former prime minister trying to innocently enjoy a day out with your family. Tell us how it feels to dance with death."

"It's absolutely alarming. We had no idea that there was a live rocket in the park. I've lived within 400 miles of this park for 30 years, and I've never seen a spacecraft take off at this particular family-friendly attraction before. It could've taken someone's eye out!"

I wrenched my eyes away from the screen and shoved my brain back into its sockets.

"Ollie…" I said slowly, trying to sound chilled out like a cheetah, "Did you have any tiny lickle inkling that the rocket was a rocket-y rocket and not just a statue-y rocket?"

Ollie looked at me aghast. "Do I look like the kind of person who has lickle inklings?! When I have inklings, you'll jolly well know about it!"

"Hmm," I said, unsure what to think. That Ollie is a wild card. You never know what he's going to do next. One minute you're eating soufflé together, the next minute he might come bursting through a door that you thought was solid but which he had spent hours replacing with an exact replica just so he could burst through it. I certainly wouldn't put any of this rocket business past him either.

Having run out of former prime ministers to interview, the news had switched over to their science correspondent.

"We have reached out to NASA for comment, and they have stated that this is probably a clear violation of international space laws and possibly poses a significant threat to global security. The Chinese government have said that it's most likely just a

weather balloon that blew off course, and clarified, "we've never even heard of space." Not wanting to miss out on this festival of statement issuing, even the cosmetics industry conglomerate "Big Cosmetics" has issued one too, as if in answer to a question no one was asking."

Our utmost concern is the safety and wellbeing of our consumers. While we understand that the rocket was meant to be a harmless attraction, we believe that the launch of such a craft poses a significant threat to public safety, on this planet and elsewhere. I mean, just on this planet. As such, we, the cosmetics industry, are calling on NASA to take immediate action and shoot down the rocket with a nuclear weapon before it leaves the Earth's atmosphere.

We understand that this action may seem extreme, and could kill a lot of people, but we believe nuking it out of the sky in a blazing fireball is the only safe way to prevent any harm. We want to reassure our customers and the public that we have nothing at all to do with this event, in any way, and there's no need to check. We are a responsible and ethical group of billion dollar companies committed to providing safe and effective cosmetics to our consumers, human or otherwise. I mean, just human. We hope that this incident serves as a reminder of the importance of responsible and safe practices when building rockets in children's play areas, and of course the necessity of a good skin care regime.

The correspondent continued,

"It is believed that the aforementioned anthropomorphic carrot was on board the rocket when it took off. Who this little vegetable spaceman is, and his mission purpose are as yet unknown, but stay tuned to Channel 819 and we'll get to the root of it."

The news bulletin ended and I turned to Ollie, who was just getting up off the floor, having decided to stay there until the news had finished to avoid further shocks. How could this be possible? Was Muncho really some kind of carrotnaut? I knew he'd been obsessed with the idea of vegetable space travel ever since the launch of Spudnik, but surely I would've noticed him undergoing ten years of training, even if it was early in the morning and I only had one eye open. Or maybe he wasn't even from Earth at all, perhaps he was one of those extra-terrestrial vegetables you never hear about. Well, kale-ien or not, he was still my friend. I rubbed my eyes, half-convinced that I was still dreaming. But no, this was really real.

The idea of NASA, or some corporate interest, shooting down the rocket filled me with dread. I didn't understand why a cosmetics conglomerate would be interested in the doings of a carrot rocket, and it made me wonder if something sinister was going to happen in Chapter 3.

At this point I would naturally have turned once more to Ollie to talk things through and work out what was going on, and break up the prose a bit with some speech, but unfortunately at that exact moment he was mown down by one of those airport shuttle buggies, and I thought I'd better give him a minute to recover physically and emotionally.

Sparing no thought for the editors of the inevitable film adaptation of this book, I couldn't help but have a conversation with myself.

> Josh: "This is insane. A carrot... as a rocket ship? How is that even possible?"

> *Inner Josh: "Well, stranger things have happened. Remember when your cat, Patricia Featherbottom, ran off to join the circus in book 1? She was a cat, with no juggling skills. How was that even possible?"*

> Josh: "Yeah, that probably should've raised some flags. But this is different. I thought the rocket statue was made of fibreglass,

which isn't known for its grace under pressure. And what does it run on, photosynthesis?!"

Inner Josh: "Who knows! Maybe it's powered by the sheer force of Muncho's determination and will to fulfil the prophecy."

Josh: "Oh, not the prophecy again. I knew you were going to say that."

Inner Josh: "But think about it. Maybe Muncho was right. Maybe there was something more that needed to happen at Carrotland. Maybe the rocket launch was it!"

Josh: "Do you mean I was meant to be on that rocket with him?"

Inner Josh: "Who are you asking? I'm you."

Josh: "Yeah, I was worried I might say that."

Bored with my inane prattling, Ollie picked himself up, dusted himself off, and suggested we try cracking on a bit in case this was as boring for the reader as it was for him. He may have had a point.

It was a perfect summer's day in Barcelona as Ollie and I walked out of Heathrow airport into a cold, rainy London afternoon. We hopped onto our horses (I always travel by horse because they're just nice, aren't they?) and set a course for the city centre. I don't know if you've ever tried to get a reindeer onto a horse, but it's not ideal, let me tell you. There were saddles and stirrups everywhere.

The news was still full of news about Muncho's extraordinary space flight, but due to the poor radio reception on our horses we were reliant on little sooty lads on cobbled street corners shouting 'extra extra! read all about it!' from under their flat caps and chimney brushes, like something out of a Jane Austen novel set in Dickensian London. It was hard to catch every word but we managed to gather a bushel of facts. It appeared that the rocket either had bedding for Lars, was full of cigars, or was writing its memoirs. Ollie had a lickle inkling that this didn't sound quite right, so we splashed out on a newspaper. The rocket, it turned out, had no bedding or cigars, but it didn't mention the memoirs so we have to assume they're in full flow. The other thing it clarified was that the rocket was heading for Mars! The newspaper also said that, thanks to intelligence from an anonymous source connected to the cosmetics industry, NASA had concluded that Muncho, my carrotty bosom buddy, was some sort of massive wrong-un. A spokesperson from Big Cosmetics was quoted on page 4, just under an unrelated picture of a cabbage:

> *"We should all now be deeply concerned about the safety of the public, given the unpredictable nature of carrots, and it's probably a good time to seriously consider panicking. We have reason to believe that Muncho, who for all we know has weapons training and no sense of proportion, poses a significant threat to our operations and to world peas. Therefore, we stand prepared to take all necessary measures to eliminate this threat. And by all necessary measures, we mean nukes. Big nukes. We cannot stress this enough. Nukes are the answer."*

We rode on in silence, feeling the storm clouds gather around us, both literally and metaphorically. It had started to rain heavily both in my soul and on my head, and I knew this was going to be a very long journey. I don't know if you've ever tried to put an anorak on a reindeer that's on a horse, but it's an absolute horror show.

3

Welcome Back, "Admiral Muncho"

28 HOURS EARLIER

Muncho was sitting alone in the rocket statue, quietly whimpering as he sang Happy Birthday to himself. Josh, his friend and confidant, his spirit guidee for the last 30 years, was gone, like hope from the hearts of millennials. And what of the prophecy? How could Josh not see there was more to be fulfilled? All, it seemed, was lost. Like Dwayne Johnson's toilet seat, he was at rock bottom, trapped and afraid.

As he finished Happy Birthday's little known seventh verse, the inside of the rocket was suddenly transformed. Out of the statue's fibreglass shell came a myriad of illuminated buttons and controls. A screen appeared and the words LAUNCH SEQENCE ACTIVATED flashed across it. Muncho noticed with annoyance that someone had mis-spelled the word sequence, but he didn't have time to dwell on that. Lots of futuristic beeping commenced and the rocket began to shake violently, like a blancmange balanced delicately on a pneumatic drill. In terrified desperation Muncho continued singing with even greater vim and vigour, clinging tightly to the edges of the rocket's single seat.

He looked around frantically, and realised with a start that the rocket was preparing to blast off into space! It seemed that Happy Birthday had been some kind of secret activation code. What were the chances of that?! Muncho could hear the screams of many former Prime Ministers, their children and dogs running away from the rocket. He wouldn't be surprised if there was some bother about this later. Suddenly the leafy boosters roared improbably to life, and he felt a surge of acceleration as the rocket lifted off the ground. The G-forces pressed against him, and he struggled to keep his eyes open as he hurtled upwards into the sky.

As he climbed higher and higher, Muncho could feel the pressure building in his ears, which was strange because Muncho doesn't have ears. His palms were slick with sweat, and his heart raced in his chest, which was also strange because although there are several vegetables with chests, everyone knows the only vegetable with a heart is an artichoke. The vibrations from the engine were so intense that he felt like he was being blended into some sort of awful healthy smoothie.

Suddenly, everything went silent, and not just because of his lack of ears. He had reached zero gravity, and Muncho felt himself floating freely inside the cabin of the rocket. He unstrapped himself from the seat and pushed off, feeling weightless and exhilarated. Weixhilarated.

Looking out of the window, Muncho saw the Earth far below, a beautiful blue and green orb with white bits. The moon was shining brightly, and he could see the stars twinkling in the darkness of space, like when you put a colander on your head and look at a torch. It was a breathtaking view, but that didn't matter to Muncho with his lack of lungs. For the next few minutes, he floated around the cabin, taking in the wonder of weightlessness. Every movement felt effortless, and he couldn't help but laugh. All those years of singing Happy Birthday to cheer himself up, and nothing, even his favourite verse (the 14th), had come close to this! But then, reality set in like a concrete trifle. He was on a fibreglass carrot-shaped rocket. He was alone, for the first time ever. He didn't have any local currency. Was this thing even air tight? Did he, a lungless anthropomorphic carrot, need oxygen to survive? And most importantly, where was he going? He longed for the answers that would come in Chapter 4. Perhaps he was about to find out more about the 'purpose' of which the prophecy had foretold. Or, said the other half of his brain, perhaps he was going to die horribly in space. However, as Muncho reflected, since this was so early in the book, it wasn't likely that anything like that would happen for a while yet.

As all these questions swirled around his mind like a lentil casserole, a console flickered to life on the control desk in front of him, picking up a distant signal from deep space. The crackly fuzz of the screen settled and Muncho found himself looking at a grinning carrot wearing an army helmet and a thick green moustache.

"Welcome back, Admiral Muncho!" the carrot exclaimed, the volume of his voice causing Muncho to jump back in his seat in alarm. He wished he had a neck brace he could put on. "Was your quest on Earth successful?" asked the voice. "Where is the world's most influential carrot?"

Muncho rubbed his temples, trying to piece together the fragments of his memory.

"What quest? What are you talking about?" he asked, confusion evident in his voice and words.

The carrot on the screen let out a heavy sigh.

"Ah. Since we've had no communication from you for thirty years, we worried this might be the case. It seems that the trauma of time travel has erased your memory.

As the moustachioed carrot spoke, Muncho suddenly felt dizzy as a rush of memories flooded his mind. The story Josh's parents used to tell about them falling in love over the carcass of a burning swan, the sound of Jordan's panicked cries every time he saw a clock, and all the worrying cat hair on the carpet all rushed back to him in a flash.

He stumbled forward, grabbing onto the console for support as the carrot continued to speak.

"Our sources indicated that Joshua Daryl Carrott was the world's most influential carrot, and so you were sent back in time to befriend and guide him up until the present, so he would be ready to come and save us."

"Josh?" Muncho queried. "You need Josh to save you?"

"Indeed, Admiral Muncho. This is very serious, and actually not that surprising given that he's the main character of this book."

"And whose idea was it to send me back in time?" asked Muncho, bamboozled by the whole thing.

"Why, yours, Admiral," said the moustachioed carrot.

Muncho shook his head in disbelief, wondering if it might explode. "I'm sorry, this is rather a lot to take in. My memory is still a bit fuzzy."

"Do you remember anything at all?" the serious carrot asked him seriously, through his serious moustache.

"My first memories are with Josh on his third birthday. I was his special best buddy, guiding him through life's struggles. I thought that was my purpose on earth. I felt fulfilled. I thought I'd done a good job, but you're saying I was sent to fulfil a greater mission, but forgot about it? Who… who are you anyway? Who am I? Who's the President? What time is lunch? Do we need milk?!"

The carrot on the screen smiled patiently.

"Let me explain. You are from an ancient race of sentient carrots called Radixicons. I am General Ammo, head of the Radixicon armed and legged forces. Our home is Mars, often insultingly called The Red Planet when it is in fact orange. It is orange because it is filled with the priceless mineral Carrotinium. NASA has been secretly studying our planet for years, but last year the cosmetics industry on Earth found that Carrotinium had miraculous anti-aging properties - it's why Radixicons never age, although we can die if we're sliced or diced, so beware falling objects. Anyway, it was with this discovery that our troubles began. In a scenario much like the plot of Avatar - but not close enough to warrant copyright concerns - the humans came to our planet to mine our precious Carrotinium and now they won't leave."

Muncho, still in a daze from all the revelations, tried to process what he had just heard. He felt like his past was slowly starting to come back to him, like a self-doubting boomerang, but there were still some details that eluded him. He took a deep breath (or he would've done if he had any lungs), and asked, "Who am I then?"

"You are the great Admiral Muncho, Glorious Leader of our heroic people!"

"And why," Muncho asked, baffled, boggled and utterly boffled, "do we need Josh, even if he is the most influential carrot in the world?"

"That answer to that is in the next chapter, so if this were a book there'd be a very good reason to keep reading" the carrot replied cryptically. "You must remember, Admiral Muncho, the fate of our entire species depends on Josh Carrott. Also, before you get here you really need to know that-" General Ammo's voice cut out, the console went dark and all was silent.

Then it sputtered to life again.

"Only joking!" said General Ammo, laughing heartily. "I was doing that thing where the thing cuts out right at the crucial moment when someone's delivering important-"

Muncho waited patiently for the General to come back, musing about how much less funny it was the second time, but this time he really did seem to have gone.

Sitting alone in the vast darkness of space, Muncho wished he could deal with the crippling weight of pressure and responsibility in some way other than by singing Happy Birthday. He wanted so much to sing-soothe his stresses away, but after what happened last time, he didn't dare.

4

THE FLASHBACK

As Muncho sat silently in the rumbling rocket, not daring to sing, he suddenly remembered something. It was like a window opening in the corner of his mind and a self-confident boomerang flying right in. Conveniently for the reader, Muncho was experiencing a flashback that would provide very necessary exposition for his current circumstances.

In his mind's eye he saw the sun shining bright on the Martian soil, and a carrot community basking in the glory of their blissful lives. They were basking here, basking there, basking all over the place. They were a contented species, living in harmony with the NASA research rovers that had landed on their planet years before.

Muncho's memories came trickling back, like a very tiny flood. He saw that it had been a time of mutual exchange and learning. The robots, Pathfinder, Curiosity Rover, and Opportunity Rover, had come in the name of science and discovery. Unlike Radixicons, who yearn for nothing in life beyond the opportunity to bask, the human race has long been known for its insatiable thirst for knowledge, its unwavering pursuit of discovery, and its ongoing quest for work-life balance.

After years of peaceful study, a NASA employee at a cocktail party in Notting Hill had accidentally let slip to a cosmetics industry executive that there was a new material on Mars which was the panacea they had so long sought: the anti-ageing miracle that was the source of the Radixicons' immortality, smooth skin and sense of general wellbeing. This is why the most common phrase on Mars is "Zero wrinkles, zero wrongkles". Soon Big cosmetics were conducting their own research

on the Orange Planet, and it wasn't long before they discovered the bountiful well of Carrotinium entombed in the core of the Radixicons' Martian home. The cosmetics industry had promised to study the life-preserving Carrotinium calmly and responsibly, and without shouting, and the carrots had welcomed them with open arms, raised eyebrows and a peculiar lack of ears. But all that changed in late 2022.

Unbeknownst to the Radixicons, the ne'er-do-wells at Big Cosmetics, led by their secretive and staggeringly naughty CEO Olaf Mursk, had long been eyeing other planets as a source of moisturising and exfoliating minerals. Now, they had surreptitiously infected NASA's rovers with an evil AI chatbot that controlled their every move. After that, any interaction the Radixicons had with the rovers would just result in pithy responses and occasionally inaccurate information.

This actually turned out to be the least of the Radixicons' concerns, because while they'd been out basking, the Chatbot-controlled NASA rovers had drawn up plans for a gigantic drill to mine Carrotinium from the planet's core. They worked at breathtaking speed and within weeks they had built a drilling complex 30 storeys high, and Big Cosmetics soon returned from Earth with an army of AI controlled drones who would guard the drill and prevent the carrots from stopping it. It was all terribly modern.

Muncho squirmed as the painful memories kept coming. He recalled his army's attempts to stop the machines, first by politely requesting, then flirting, and finally with saucy dancing, but to no avail. Over time they realised that the evil AI Chat Bot, like all overlords, was becoming smug. It started toying with them. The irreverent, self-confident, condescending tone they all initially admired had become unbearable, but it also provided an opportunity. After months of research Percepto the Orange, the Radixicon's pre-eminent wise mind, convened the planet's premier scientific society, the Council of Clever Carrots, and revealed his grand plan. The chat bot's hubris, he explained, could be its Achilles elbow. All they had to do was convince the bot to show off more and more, until one day it might reveal something about itself that they could exploit.

Muncho's memory fast-forwarded past a few days in which nothing much happened besides basking, and into his mind's eye strode a tall, confident looking carrot wearing pince-nez spectacles and bermuda shorts, who stepped forward to stand before the machine.

"Excuse me, O evil one. Big fan. Big fan. Great hair. " said the carrot, who had a tendency to simply list everything he could see whenever he was nervous.

"Big Fan. Swivel chair. Kettle. My name's Cruncho, Minister for Drill Destruction. I was chatting with the lads in my spin class and they said they don't think you're as indestructible as you make out.

The machine emitted a low rumble and eyed him evilly with its evil eyes.

Cruncho continued, "Toilet brush. Feather boa. They bet me that if you gave us a clue we could work out how to make you shut down. Bunion cream. Of course, I said we'd never know because you'd be too much of a cowardy custard to actually do it…"

The machine glared and scowled, scared and glowed, and then the evil thing made a beep-boop noise and spat something angrily from its printer.

Cruncho gingerly stepped forward and took the paper. It contained an ASCII drawing of a boxing glove and four lines of text, in the form of a riddle. He decided to ignore the boxing glove and focus on the text.

Despite your carrot army, you haven't got a hope.
If your question's 'can we win?' the answer's surely 'nope'.
The only way to stop us, and rid Mars of this blight
Is to search in every corner, for the one who holds the light.
I know this is a riddle, but let me be quite clear:
Finding a great carrot would be an excellent idea.
At the risk of getting boring, and repeating like a parrot,
Your best way to avoid being horribly murdered is to find the world's
most influential carrot.

The carrots were stumped. They had never encountered anything like this before. They were a peace-loving species, more skilled in basking than solving puzzles and riddles.

"Mmm, this is quite the pickle," mused Muncho, scratching his head. "And the last line doesn't scan very well, which is a little odd for a superintelligent machine."

Sensing that a good pun would lift everyone's spirits, he continued, "Lettuce all take a moment to think about its meaning, and try not to turnip your noses at any possibilities."

Cruncho raised a carrot-like finger.

"What is it, Cruncho?" asked Muncho.

"I'm not sure, but maybe if we find the most influential carrot among us, they will be the metaphorical key to the literal problem?"

There was a murmur of agreement in the gathered ranks. The riddle certainly did seem to be heavily implying that. But everybody knew that Muncho was the most influential carrot among them, that's why he was their de facto leader, much to the annoyance of their most decorated soldier, De Facto. A shorter carrot with a shocking pink afro and a tendency to butcher aphorisms hopped forward.

"Just a minute," said Buncho, "the riddle says the world's most influential carrot. But we're not from the world, we're from Mars. I think we need to grab the bull by its knees, pull our socks off, fall over backwards and look on Earth for our saviour!"

Muncho grinned, clapping Buncho on the back. Turning to his right, he addressed his Chief of Intelligence, a large carrot with a great big bushy beard, and a countenance to match.

"Huncho, we need you to find the most influential carrot on Earth. You have all of our resources at your disposal, because unless we find this carrot of colossal influence, these machines are going to steal all of the Carrotinium from our core and we'll be doomed! Doomed! Whatever you do, don't lettuce down!"

The carrots cheered in unison. They'd heard that pun before, but they knew that with determination, courage, and the power of love on their side, they were sure to succeed. In just a few chapters' time they would surely be returning to their salad days.

Muncho made his way to a large console in the middle of the room and commanded it to turn on by bellowing the magic word. "BUTTRESS!" he yelled, at the top of his non-existent lungs. The screen instantly sprang to life, and Muncho stepped aside to allow his henchman to do the boring worky bit. Huncho took to the keyboard with the skills of Mozart, and performed an Ask Leaves search for "Influential, excellent, and downright handsome carrots". After scrolling through 110 pages of questionable AI generated images and erotic fiction, Huncho stopped and stared. On page 111 was an image like no other. Checking momentarily that he hadn't accidentally searched for "greatest book cover in history", he turned the screen to face the throng of eager faces. Some gasped. Others whimpered in awe, as they beheld the most beautiful book any of them had ever seen.

"Egadzooks," whispered Muncho reverently.

"It's described as 'an incredible autobiography of a man called Joshua Daryl Carrott with a vegetable spirit guide called Muncho'", said Huncho.

The room fell silent as they skimmed the exquisitely written and very reasonably priced autobiography (whose writers are available for commissions). The descriptions of Josh's carrot companion, his love of the song Happy Birthday, his lack of ears, and overall joie de vivre were unmistakably those of their Commander in Leaf.

"But how can this be you, Admiral Muncho?" asked Huncho, "this is 30 years ago, in Caterham, England, Planet Earth! And besides, in Josh Carrott's account you are imaginary and yet you stand before us, really real," he added, prodding his commanding officer gently, just to be sure.

"This is a paradox in the time-space continuum," came a deep voice from the corner.

Without anyone noticing, Percepto the Orange had entered the briefing room, dressed in salopettes and carrying a riding crop.

"What you are witnessing is a potential actuality, untethered from the quantum realm - a little understood consequence of time travel. When someone alters the course of history from the future, they are both there and not there, real and unreal. Two universes overlap simultaneously, like ham and cheese in a sandwich. This creates experiential abnormalities, such as a young boy seeing a carrot friend that no one else can see, and us being able to reference a book that won't exist for 30 years. My hunch is that what is written in Josh Carrott's book is a course of events we are bound by the laws of physics to fulfil. In a sense, we have already fulfilled them. We must send Admiral Muncho back in time to befriend Josh Carrott. The prophecy in Chapter 23 of his bestselling book makes plain that he is the influential carrot we seek."

There was a silence so quiet it was barely audible, as the crowd of carrots digested Percepto's words.

"Well, that's clear as water," said Buncho. "Fire up the time machine!"

"We have a time machine?!" asked Cruncho, confused.

"Yes. Top secret stuff, above your paygrade Cruncho. Terrible operational security, Buncho!" shouted General Ammo as he opened a vault door to reveal a really whizz-bang-fantastic time machine. To the untrained eye it looked just like a regular time machine, only shaped like a carrot.

"Why does everything have to be shaped like a carrot?" asked Cruncho.

"FOR INSPIRATION!!" everyone yelled in unison.

"This thing is the absolute dog's pajamas," said Buncho. "Like most time machines, this baby is powered by music. Sing Happy Birthday to launch, then you simply work your way back through the music of the eras until you reach the year you want. You'll need these," he said, handing Muncho a large number of vinyl records. "We haven't got it to work on MP3 yet. Haven't had time, ironically."

"Wow," said Muncho, surpfused. "Like the iceberg said of the Titanic, I did not see this coming." Then a faraway look crossed his eyebrows. "It's going to be a long, long journey through the early 2000s."

"Remember", said Buncho solemnly, "In order to appear on Josh's third birthday as his autobiography says you will, you're aiming for May 1992, so slow down when you hear Boom! Shake the Room by Will Smith and Jazzy Jeff. If you get to Rhythm is a Dancer you've gone too far. Oh, and be careful of the Do They Know It's Christmas time loop. They released that thing like eight times and the machine can get confused. If it does, whack it with this."

So saying, he handed Muncho a screwdriver.

"And whatever you do, be very very careful not to go too fast, or you're at grave risk of - "

"Get in there!" interrupted Puncho, the Radixicon's resident enforcer, shoving the Admiral through the time machine's carrot-shaped door and completely ruining Buncho's hilarious joke.

Inside the machine Muncho got to his feet, his non-existent heart pounding with excitement. Looking around, he couldn't help but smile at his comrades' ingenuity. The tiny vessel was a masterpiece of technology, with shiny buttons, blinking lights, and a magnificently carved celeriac gramophone. It was a lot bigger than it looked from the outside, and the interior was beautifully painted in obscure colours. The high domed ceiling of the control room was a shade of vermillion that Muncho thought offset the amaranth light shades wonderfully. He must get the number of the designer, he thought. Down a corridor to the left there were sleeping quarters and a kitchen, and beyond the toilet block he thought he saw a sign saying 'Petting Zoo'. Overhead a fan whirled lazily, and out on the veranda a soft breeze played through the jacaranda trees, causing the rocking chairs to creak ominously. Somewhere in the distance, just beyond the bayou, a banjo played. Muncho took a deep breath, his fingers hovering over the stylus, and prayed for deliverance.

"Here goes nothing," he whispered to himself as he began to quietly hum Happy Birthday.

Immediately, the time machine roared to life, and Muncho felt his non-existent stomach drop as the floor beneath him shook. His colleagues, Cruncho, Buncho, Puncho, Huncho and General Ammo, watched in amazement as the carrot-shaped vessel disappeared in a flash of orange light.

"Well I'll be julienned," said Buncho. "I didn't think it would actually work."

"Watch your language!" ordered General Ammo, shocked to the core. There really was no call for such vulgarity.

Muncho let the stylus drop into the groove on the first of a stack of 45s, and held on tight as the time machine hurtled through space and time, through the entire back catalogues of Ed Sheeran and Miley Cyrus, then the Spice Girls and Oasis. He could feel the rush of the wind as he sped through the decades, his imaginary heart beating in time to Run DMC's It's Like That, and then Haddawy's timeless hit 'What is Love?' It was all going rather well, Muncho thought, until he reached 1993 and Thousand by Moby came on. Muncho remembered, too late, that this little known B-side had officially the fastest beat in musical history. Muncho grabbed desperately at the needle, but the machine was already going too fast and he was flung against the back wall of the cockpit, momentarily forgetting that he was supposed to be weightless. A sudden burst of energy pulsed through the ship, coursing through everything in it, including Muncho, and he felt consciousness slipping from him.

Coming to again halfway through Take That's Could it be Magic, Muncho realised that he had lost all memory of his mission, his identity, and his purpose for being there. He would be a carrot with eyebrows but no past, wandering the Earth in a strange, new era. Only a name kept floating around his head, "Joshua Daryl Carrott". He decided to track down this mysterious protagonist and see what happened. Fortunately for Muncho, Josh had been winning awards left, right and centre since the day he was born, so this wouldn't be half as difficult as it sounds.

As the needle slipped into the run out groove and the time machine slowed to a stop, the Earth of the past came into focus. The streets were lined with cars from a different era, the just-opened Disneyland Paris gleamed like a freshly glazed pain-au-raisin, and over 4,000 miles away American TV audiences were sitting down to watch Beverly Hills 90210. This last realisation worried Muncho, who liked to keep up to date with popular culture - what if he couldn't follow the plot after missing the first 90209 episodes?

5

Josh Influences His Way To Mars

Back home in London I, Joshua Daryl Carrott, was back in first person mode and having an emotional crisis. I liked to keep a TV on full blast in every room of the house due to my lifelong fear of silence, but now, for the first time, it had begun to be more of a curse than a blessing. In the shower I watched the news cycle churn out a constant stream of updates about Muncho's journey to Mars, but it's a long way and nothing much seemed to be happening. I was relieved, on day four of Muncho's extraordinary expedition, when I opened a cutlery drawer and the TV inside informed me that Muncho was in slightly less danger of fiery doom than he had been. The governments of the world had signed a peace accord called the Carrot-Human Understanding Mandate, or CHUM for short, and almost everyone agreed that total annihilation might be a teeny bit of an overreaction. NASA and Big Cosmetics had been convinced to stand down their nukes for fear of enraging the Empire from Star Wars, in case they existed, which they honestly might as well at this point.

Then, about a week after Muncho's unexpected exit, I opened the fridge to get some crème fraîche and the TV on the middle shelf showed a rather cold looking news reader with another urgent update:

BREAKING NEWS:
Intergalactic Terrorist Muncho Threatens Global Security!

"Reports coming in from NASA indicate that the mysterious extraterrestrial vegetable known as Muncho has set foot on Mars, and in response Big Cosmetics have released another statement banging on about how the diminutive daredevil poses a direct threat to global security. Their spokesmodel said:

> *The motives of the illegal stowaway carrot known as Muncho the Naughty are still totally unknown, but our sources suggest that he definitely must be gathering resources to use in a devastating attack. It's the only thing that makes any sense. His powers are probably formidable, and his determination almost certainly shows no sign of weakening. Also he's unquestionably armed to the teeth and desperate to kill everyone. It seems that Muncho the Awful is hell-bent on making an impact on the entire world, literally.*
>
> *We- I mean, our partners at NASA have been working tirelessly to locate Muncho the Dreadful, but all attempts have so far been unsuccessful. A NASA spokesmodel described the task as 'like looking for a needle in a haystack, only the needle is a carrot, and the haystack is Mars. You get the picture'. It is essential that Muncho the Potentially Murderous be located and apprehended before he can cause any further worry on top of that which he's already wrought in our hearts and minds.*
>
> *The public is advised to remain vigilant and take all necessary precautions to protect themselves against this intergalactic threat which 100% exists, trust us. If any amateur astronomers have any information regarding Muncho the Harbinger of the Apocalypse's whereabouts, please contact authorities immediately.*
>
> *Remember, Stay safe! Stay alert! Stay moisturised!*

"That's all we have for now, but stay tuned for all the latest news, weather and lounge jazz throughout the day."

The news reader rang off.

I turned away from the TV and closed the fridge, which had started bonging at me for leaving the door open for too long. How anyone is supposed to enjoy watching TV with bonging left, right and centre is beyond me. Anyway, despite Big Cosmetics' attempts to smear my bosom pal, I wasn't falling for it. I knew the carrot they depicted wasn't the Muncho the Very Nice that I knew. I knew Muncho, and I also knew that when you know you know a person, you know you know them, you know? I was determined to make amends with Muncho, but what could I do? Sure, I was a good looking guy, the Caterham region Boggle champion 1997-9 and one heck of a YouTuber, but how was I going to use any of that? I slumped into a giant hand chair and pulled my best glum face, in case anyone was watching. Suddenly, a metaphorical light flickered inside my brain (my metaphorical wiring has never been quite right) and I had a brilliant idea. There was only one thing for it; it was time to assemble the wives for another thrilling adventure! I called Ollie and Gabie (in that order) and reminded them that as characters in this book it was about time they started pulling their weight. Ollie said a lot of very unhelpful things such as 'gadzooks!' 'by jingo!' 'billy bally bungo!' and other codswallop. Gabie, as ever, was a lot more attractive and useful, and revealed that she'd signed us up for a brand experience with a bunch of other influencers. Usually these things are fun enough, but don't exactly solve major life problems, but this one seemed different. Apparently a large anonymous cosmetics conglomerate with a PR problem had invited us to visit one of their factories. The email said to report to Spaceport Cornwall the following day, destination: MARS. What a stroke of luck, I thought; I could rescue Muncho from certain death, and it would be on someone else's dime. It all felt fortuitously fortunate. Almost a little too fortuitously fortunate. But fortunately, it would turn out to be just the right amount of fortuneity. Phew.

***

I've always said that travel is a thing best done in a tearing hurry, and so it was that we met the following day, late as usual, on top of the giant clock at St Swithin's station. Gabie and Ollie were already there when I arrived.

"What ho!" I said, chipperly.

"Great scott!" Gabie yelled theatrically, startling my owl. "We've no time for idle chit-chat, we need to shake a leg, lest we miss our rocket!"

"Cripes-a-rumba, you're right as usual!" I cried, shaking both legs and startling Ollie, who was deep in thought about his next hairstyle.

"I'm thinking of getting a beehive," he said, with wild eyes.

"You'll have to mullet over," I told him, "We've got to get to Cornwall tout suite! Allez!"

Moving at the speed of humans, we leapt into our carriages and charged at the wall between platforms 9a and 9c. Crashing headlong into the wall was never fun, but it did help to wake me up. Gathering our scattered belongings and ignoring the crowd of bemused commuters, we turned in the direction of Cornwall and ran like the clappers.

As you'd expect if you thought about it for even a second, there was quite a crowd lining the small road that led to the Spaceport, and as the paparazzi lights flashed and reporters shouted questions, we saw two of our fellow social media stars step out of their carriages and onto the red carpet. Pake and Pogan Laul needed no introduction. Two brothers, four legs, one surname, six packs, seven swans a-swimming and five gold rings, they were two of the most popular influencers in the galaxy, with a pair of egos the size of Neptune (or perhaps two healthy senses of self in a world that tells us all we suck, who can say?) They were dressed to the nines, in sharp tuxedos which sparkled in the lights. They smiled for the cameras, waved to the cheering fans, and did a spot of light boxing as they made their way towards the entrance of the launch pad.

Next came PSI and his fellow YouTube crew of Margin Misters, making age appropriate jokes and being uncontroversial (like this boring book once the character names and jokes have been approved by our lawyers). PSI threw a few punches in the air as he made his way down the carpet. Fans cheered and clapped, caught up in the excitement of the moment. Reporters shouted questions at him, but he simply smiled and waved, like an absolute pro.

Once the inevitable interviews and selfies were over, we boarded the rocket that would be our home for the next several hours. A frisson of nervous energy tweaked my excitement glands as I strapped myself in for the adventure, both literally and metaphorically. I don't know if you know, because I don't like to talk about it, but I drive a Tesla, so I'm used to exciting journeys. But even that paled into insignificance when compared with the out-of-this-world trip that lay before me. After all, how often do you get to travel to another planet with a gaggle of social media influencers, all of whom are packed into a spacecraft with questionable snack choices and a dubious karaoke machine? And would you want to? Either way, I was already looking forward to saying it was the best space journey I'd ever had, but not yet. The trick with these things is timing.

A voice on the intercom told us to stop boxing and fasten our seatbelts, and next thing I knew we were hurtling away from the spaceport like buttered toast off a plate. We soon settled into the stereotypical activities you'd expect from our personalities. Pake and Pogan Laul started a vlog documenting the entire adventure, complete with overly enthusiastic introductions and an impromptu dance party. PSI, never one to shy away from a challenge, tried to organise a boxing competition, but couldn't make the weight categories work in zero gravity.

Gabie had discovered the karaoke machine and, fueled by a combination of boredom and space snacks, decided to perform a heartfelt rendition of "Rocket Man" no fewer than seventeen times. It turns out the first time was the charm.

Around the halfway point I declared the journey to be the best space journey I'd ever had, at which point Ollie, who was still debating whether a Mohican would be the most aerodynamic hairstyle for the journey, whipped out a bingo card and crossed something off. He's so funny sometimes.

As we approached the world that we still knew as the Red Planet (on account of not having read this book yet), the excitement in the spacecraft was palpable, so I palped it. Everyone's thoughts turned to their plans once we landed. Pake and Pogan Laul were busy planning a Mars-themed prank for their channel, while Gabie was already brainstorming ideas for a Martian-inspired casserole. Ollie, having finally settled on a French bob, was instagramming the heck out of himself with the Martian landscape in the background, a true pioneer of interplanetary hair fashion. He's so funny, all the time.

As the spacecraft began its descent onto the Martian surface, our excitement grew exponentially, like compound interest or bacteria under The Rock's toilet seat. We could see the red sands of Mars creeping closer through the windows, although it looked a lot more orange than any of us expected. While the onboard computer counted down the final moments until touchdown, we braced ourselves for impact, gripping onto anything we could find as the retro rockets fired, kicking up a cloud of orange dust around us. It was quite good, really.

I looked out of the six-sided window at the desolate landscape we were about to call home. I'd never visited somewhere with so little atmosphere before - well, not since a school trip to Grimsby in Year 5. The two places were more similar than I was expecting - a barren, featureless wasteland covered in the ruins of past glories, and lots of orange people wandering around. But hang on, those weren't people, they were carrots! Thousands of carrots as far as the eye could see, all basking their bottoms off. Could this be where Muncho came from, I wondered, and realised with a pang of guilt that in 30-odd years of friendship I'd never thought to ask. To be fair, I have been busy.

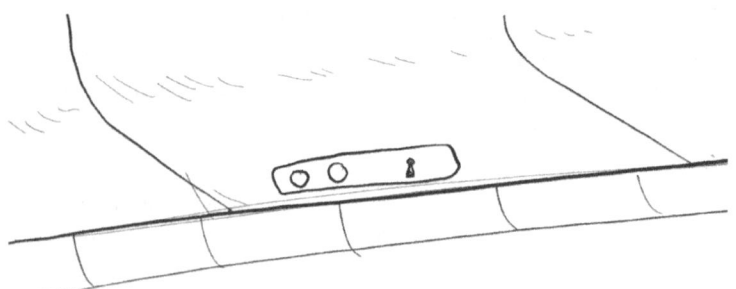

With a final jolt, the spacecraft touched down at the Martian spaceport, and a series of alien sounding beeps and boops confirmed our arrival. We all applauded the almost perfect landing - not quite impeccable, but certainly not peccable as far as I could tell. We also congratulated the pilot for having a truly magnificent moustache, which I think she appreciated. We looked around at one another, our eyes wide with a mixture of relief and awe - relawe. It felt a bit like destiny, which I'd never believed in before, but now wholeheartedly did. At any rate, we had made it – we were on Mars!

6

Operation Extraction Distraction

14 AND A HALF MINUTES EARLIER (LET'S CALL IT 15)

Fortunately for Muncho, our intrepid protagonist, who we last saw hurtling through space in Chapter 3 and feeling somewhat iffy, the carrot rocket turned out to be fully equipped with autopilot which took him directly to the Radixicons' Martian space base. So, while you were thoroughly enjoying Chapters 4 and 5 (weren't they good!) our hero managed to arrive and be reinstated as the rebel carrots' leader. Let's rejoin the action!

Deep inside the Radixicon base, Admiral Muncho listened intently as his junior officers filled him in on the latest intel: A spaceship jam-packed with influencers was on its way to the main spaceport to promote the latest anti-aging cream from a big cosmetics company. Nothing unusual there, he thought. Most of them seemed to be boring old boxers of one sort or another, but the description of a tall, handsome, multilingual influencer sounded a lot like Josh, his best buddy and bosom pal! The one person he could always rely on, except for that one time recently in Chapter 1 where he had abandoned him like a sack of old boots. Muncho felt a surge of emotion welling up inside him, despite having no heart. He couldn't believe that Josh had risked everything to come and save him. His eyes filled with tears as he realised just how lucky he was to have such a loyal and devoted friend, most of the time. But this was no time for emotion, that could wait for 45 minutes.

The intel suggested that upon arrival on Mars, Josh and the others would be taken on a tour of the drilling facility, and it occurred to Muncho that this might provide the Radixicons with the chance they needed to extract him without anyone noticing. A reverent hush fell over the command room as Muncho rubbed his chin, deep in thought.

"Okay, here's what we'll do," he said finally. "We'll create a distraction that Josh will recognise as a signal to make his escape, and use the commotion to extract him in Dr Wizzo's patented carrot car. We shall call it Operation Extraction Distraction."

Everyone cheered Muncho's clever wordplay, and agreed it was the best plan they'd ever heard that morning.

Buoyed by the prospect of saving their planet and not dying in a horrible fiery inferno, the rebels sprang into action, poring over Josh's best selling autobiography, which he definitely wrote all of, for clues as to what kind of signal their saviour would recognise. But time was of the essence, so it really had to be something from Chapter 1. Cruncho was the fastest reader, so he was the first to reach page 3, and the beautiful description of Josh's parents' first meeting. Cruncho, normally one of the more stoic carrots, fought back tears as he read aloud to the gathered throng the story of love and wildfowl that had moved over 15,000 readers so far.

…at that moment a train came hurtling into the station and ran over the swan's smouldering remains. My parent's romance was kindled as the glowing embers hovered gently on the breeze like confetti.

Cruncho turned from the screen to hide his face. It was the most beautiful thing he'd ever read, but it still wasn't time for emotion, that would come in 38 minutes.

General Ammo, whose moustache had gone droopy from all the crying he was pretending he hadn't done, suggested the best way to create a diversion might be by setting fire to a large swan of some kind. Buncho thought he'd seen one in the cafeteria, but after a thorough search of the base the carrots were forced to concede that, unbelievably, there were no swans to be found anywhere in their Martian home.

"What are we going to do?!" cried Buncho in desperation. "We haven't a cat in heaven's chance."

"Scones!" Suggested Luncho. "There's nothing a scone can't solve when you're in a jam."

"Cones!" Offered Huncho, who was always looking for an excuse to set up a perimeter and secure the area.

"A map of Cologne!" shouted Cruncho, who was nervously examining the wall.

"WAIT!"

The room fell suddenly silent. From the back of the gathered crowd rose a bearded carrot wearing glasses and a dirty lab coat.

"We may have no swan, but we do have a baby goose!" he boomed. "By an unbelievable stroke of fortune, our Speculative Developments department has spent the past nine years building Mars' biggest wooden statue of a young water bird, and it's just about ready!"

Muncho beamed. It couldn't be more perfect! Well, it could, but not much.

Muncho, Buncho, Cruncho, Puncho, Luncho and Huncho followed Dr Wizzo into his cavernous workshop, trembling with anticipation. As they entered the messiest room they'd ever seen, one thing really caught their attention. Before them stood a mighty wooden statue of Ryan Gosling. Muncho hung his head in despair. It was certainly beautiful, but it was a long way from the giant bird they'd originally been aiming for. "Oh, giblets." He said. Their goose was well and truly cooked.

The actor was depicted in a heroic pose, his arms outstretched towards the infinite expanse of space. Perhaps, once aflame, Muncho thought, they might look more like wings. Perhaps if Josh was only using one eye… and looking at it through a frosted window, on a foggy night. Perhaps if he'd developed cataracts, and was wearing his space helmet back to front. Despite the obvious shortcomings of the statue, Muncho had to admit it was a thing of beauty - incredibly detailed,

with every contour of Ryan's chiselled yet approachable bone structure captured perfectly in the wood. It looked nicely flammable too.

As they gazed up at the statue, Muncho and his chums felt a sense of inspiration and wonder, or insponder. It reminded them of the infinite possibilities that lay beyond their world, and the importance of exploring and understanding the mysteries of the universe. It also reminded them of freedom, and the potential of a hope renewed, like a phoenix rising from the ashes, in much the same way that a dead swan couldn't. But more than anything it reminded them of Ryan Gosling. It wasn't ideal, but there was no time to build another one before the next chapter. Also, happily it was on nice big roving wheels. It was Mars, after all, and on Mars roving really is key.

"Well, there's no time like the future." said Buncho. "The time has come when we must throw caution to the sun, bite the bully, and put our best foot upwards."

"That's right," said Muncho, buoyed by Buncho's rousing words. "Dr Wizzo, Can you give me a number crunch real quick?"

"I'm coming up with forty-four point four four, repeating of course, percentage chance of survival." said Dr Wizzo solemnly.

"I like those odds!" said Muncho, who'd never been particularly good at maths. "Let's do this! Leeee-"

"Let me just stop you there, for copyright reasons," said Dr Wizzo. "We can't afford a lawsuit right now."

"Oh, fine. In that case, GERONIMOOOO!" yelled Muncho, punching the air, in clear defiance of a nearby sign which stated that the air had a right to work without fear of violence.

The brave band of carrots, now feeling more buoyed than an airbed in the Dead Sea, began to push the roving Gosling out of the laboratory doors and into the night. They moved silently past the safe perimeter of their own base, and out into the planet's dark, desolate terrain, their movements slow and deliberate as they pushed together as one. It took several hours, and most of it wasn't anything to fax home about, but basically they survived the snows of Rivendale, avoided the boglins in the mines of Murder, and made it over Mount Gloom before rush hour, so it went pretty well.

Emerging from the Chamber of Public Knowledge, Muncho signalled for quiet, and the army slowed as the top of the ominous enemy lair came into view.

"This is it, friends." said Muncho from atop a boulder. In there we should find Josh, who we need to kidnap in order to save our planet."

"We know, Admiral Muncho, we literally made this plan with you this afternoon," chorused the carrots impatiently. "Now quit the exposition and let's crack on with it!"

Muncho surveyed the plucky bunch. They were pinning all their hopes on this plan. Would Josh recognise the Gosling? Were they just living in lala land or would this actually work? They had drive, they had notebooks full of plans, they had the first man to be set alight in place of a swan. Perhaps it was crazy, stupid, love of their planet, but they had a feeling that the plan was so good that, big, short, wide or long, it would succeed, like Barbie dolls, in terms of market dominance.

"Seriously Admiral, stop making jokes in your internal monologue, and let's get in there." said General Ammo, who was keen to bash some heads together.

Muncho signalled for the group to advance on the facility. Electing for the easiest option, they wheeled the giant Gosling through the front door and approached the ticket kiosk, where they purchased tickets for the 6:30 tour.

A robot guide appeared precisely late, and introduced himself as Manuel Override. Muncho had a sneaking suspicion this was going to be relevant later, so made a mental note of it in his mental notebook.

"Follow me please." said Manuel, looking suspiciously at the group. "Do not touch anything, or I will force myself to shoot you."

So saying, he led the carrots through an archway and into the first of many tedious rooms full of boring things. Even Muncho, who had undergone rigorous boredom training for this mission by watching every Fast and Furious movie one after another, couldn't handle the banality and drifted off for long periods, which at least saves us having to listen to any of it.

After what felt like hours (but was in fact only an hour and 58 minutes), the tour reached the Great Hall, and the rebel plan swung into action. Belcho, the noisiest carrot Mars had ever produced, ran to a corner and let out a blood curdling burp which rattled the windows and caused all the security bots to swivel in his direction. Quick as a flash that lasted about five seconds, the others pushed the giant Ryan Gosling into the centre of the room.

The robots, who were not programmed to be suspicious of human forms, paid no heed to this new addition, and couldn't know that it was stuffed to the gills with firelighters, kindling, and inflammatory rhetoric. The carrots started the countdown sundial between Ryan's legs and ran like the clappers. Manuel, who was more preoccupied with making sure his group spent big in the gift shop, failed to notice several guerrilla carrots melting into the shadows of the Great Hall like ice cream in a hot car. Muncho couldn't help but feel a sense of pride in his team. They had carried off something truly remarkable, and he knew now that they were capable of achieving anything they set their minds to, like Ryan. All they could do now was wait, the sundial ticking down and the nearby ascending lifts acting as a perfect metaphor for their mood.

7

The Briefing

Beknownst to the Radixicons, at that precise moment the ship of influencers was docking at the spaceport and disgorging its quarry, like a very efficient actual quarry. Buncho had hacked the security cameras and the carrots watched as Josh, Ollie, Gabie, Pake and Pogan Laul, and PSI stepped out onto the orange welcome carpet, their eyes wide with awnder. The carrots looked on with bemusement as the influencers began documenting their experiences, snapping selfies and live-streaming their reactions for their fans back on Earth.

Soon the group were met by a robotic representative from Big Cosmetics, who introduced herself as Iris Scanna, and greeted them with a fixed smile and an uncomfortable air of having something to hide. Josh and Ollie could sense that something was amiss, but because of all the security barriers they couldn't quite reach to put their finger on what it might be.

As the influencers were led through the labyrinthine corridors of the facility, Iris regaled them with tales of the valuable resources that were being extracted from the Martian soil. The group, moved to tears by the sheer tedium of it all, pretended to marvel at the state-of-the-art machinery, the scale of the operation, and the incredible progress that was being made in the name of smooth skin. However, as they ventured deeper into the heart of the building, they began to grow increasingly uneasy. Josh had a nagging suspicion that there was more to this facility than met either of his eyes, and he couldn't shake the feeling that he

was on the verge of discovering something truly important, something that could change the course of history forever. Or perhaps he was just hungry, that was usually it. Iris announced that the tour was nearly over, and that the last room left was the Great Hall. She punched a code into the keypad next to a pair of giant oak doors and glided through them.

Just as Muncho's band of mercenaries had planned, the moment the influencers entered the cavernous Great Hall they were discombobulated by the sight of a giant statue of Ryan Gosling, which rolled gently forward before bursting into flames.

"What shall we do now?!" cried Ollie helplessly, like a woman in a movie.

"Follow my lead!" shouted Gabie decisively, like a man in a movie. "We need fire extinguishers to extinguish the fire!" And off they ran down the corridor.

The Lauls and PSI, eager to prove themselves, immediately started raining down punches on the carcass of the giant statue in a bid to suffocate the flames, leaving Josh momentarily alone. After musing for several minutes about the oddity of a flaming Gosling, something in his subconscious whispered to his brain how much the situation would be improved by the presence of a fire officer or a police fighter, a hurtling train and true love. With a jolt of realisation, something clicked in Josh's mind and he recognised the burning Gosling as the signal he didn't even know he'd been waiting for. It had to be Muncho! Quick as a twelve second flash, he slipped away from the group and hid behind a giant pot plant to plan his next move. He was not there for anti-wrinkle cream after all (although he was starting to need it), he was on a rescue mission.

Meanwhile Admiral Muncho and his team had been waiting for Josh, ready to whisk him away to safety. As he crouched behind the pot plant Josh suddenly heard a screech of tyres and looked up to see a carrot racing car emerge from the shadows on the other side of the hall and head straight for him, coming to a halt just 200 metres from his nose.

"Jump in!" called Muncho, and Josh didn't need to be told twice. "Jump in!" said Muncho again, for he didn't know this. Josh did as he was told and jumped into the carrot car just in time to see the Gosling statue explode and crumple to the ground, with the Lauls and PSI jubilantly declaring themselves the winners on points.

As the car screeched out of the main entrance of the facility and disappeared into the night, Muncho and his team were all smiles, proud of their daring and successful mission. They had saved Josh, and they had done it with a touch of humour, a dash of absurdity and a dollop of derring-do. It was just another day in the wild and wonderful world of Muncho and his rebels. One day, thought Muncho, someone should write a book about all this.

"It would also work well as a TV mini-series," pointed out Cruncho.

Back at base, Josh and Muncho embraced in a warm, emotional reunion, both of them overjoyed to be reunited after experiencing the perfect amount of danger and drama for a bestselling book.

"Thank you for coming, Josh," Muncho said, reluctantly pulling away from the embrace. "You've saved more carrots than you realise today. You are the answer to the riddle that can deactivate the drill."

Josh raised an eyebrow, confused. "Riddle? Drill? The? Answer? Can? To? Are? Deactivate? You? That? What are you talking about?"

Muncho explained everything. "...so you see, Big Cosmetics are really quite awful, and their greed is going to destroy our whole planet! The riddle seems to be asking for the world's most influential carrot, which has to be you! I was actually sent to Earth to bring you here but my memory of this mission was lost during time travel. So we need to get you into the mainframe. We believe only you can gain root access."

Josh looked doubtful. "But I've never done anything like this before, Muncho, you know that. The closest thing I've done is asking Gabie to marry me, which you have to admit, is pretty different. Where the heck is Gabie, anyway?"

"She's probably still alive," said Muncho reassuringly. "And if not, we'll get you a new one."

With this, Muncho walked over to the central console and jabbed at some buttons in a seemingly random way. A screen lowered from the ceiling and some letters began to appear. It looked like a language, Josh thought. It was. It was English, so he had no problem understanding it.

[OPERATION 'GUARANTEED SUCCESS': INTEL BRIEFING]

Objective: To gain access to the mainframe, and disable the giant drill that is relentlessly harvesting Carrotinium from the planet's core, like a pesky mole.

Plan of Action:

Our mission will be divided into six steps, like a short staircase, as outlined below. Stealtho will have overall command of the mission, with different teams stepping in according to their talents.

Step 1 - Infiltration

Huncho will lead a covert infiltration team to gain entrance to the facility. They will be armed with EMPeas and other stealth-based weaponry, as well as specialised hacking equipment, like axes. Think Ocean's Eleven, but not too hard for copyright reasons.

Step 2 - Mainframe Access

Once inside, Buncho's team must navigate through various security measures in order to reach the mainframe and turn off the facility's security so we can get to the drill. This includes bypassing cameras, motion detectors, and other technological defences. Mission Impossible, basically.

Step 3 - Cafeteria

Luncho, your time to shine. The cafeteria is located on the same floor as the drill room. In order to access it, we will need to navigate a complicated maze of air vents and crawl spaces in order to avoid detection. This room is vitally important. It holds no strategic relevance to the plan, but we'll be hungry by this time and we'll need a boost. This is probably like Maizerunner, I don't know, I haven't seen it.

Step 4 - Drill Room

Once the security mainframe is down and we've had sandwiches, we must locate the drill room. This is where the drill is located, as well as all its components and controls. This is where Puncho's team comes in to disable the drill and render it inoperable. Anybody see 2003's The Core? No? Never mind.

Step 5 - The Core

This is where the drill is attached directly to the planet's core. Having disabled the drill in Step 4, Cruncho's team will move in to destroy it, just like in one of the good Star Wars movies, and thus we will save the planet.

Step 6 - Tea and cake

Jammo will be waiting for our glorious return with a selection of cakes, scones, and crumpets. Tea and hearty slaps on the back will be provided to any survivors, just like that bit in War and Peace where they've disabled an evil machine.

[END OF OPERATION BRIEFING]

Muncho, who had read this before so wasn't really very interested, had been standing in the corner humming verse 18 of Happy Birthday. As the briefing concluded and the lights came back up he walked over to Josh. Standing on a chair in order to look him in the eye, Muncho said sincerely, "I just want you to know that I love you. No matter what happens, no matter where we go or how far apart we are, I will always love you like a brother."

Josh smiled. "I love you too, buddy. You've been there for me through thick and thin, long and short, up and down, round and round, and back again, and I know I can always count on you. I'm sorry I let you down in New Zealand. No matter what happens in the next chapter, I'll always be there to catch you when you fall."

Muncho nodded his head in solemn agreement and gave Josh a big hug. It was beautiful, you should have been there. At that moment, a loud and ominous rumble came from the planet's core. Warnings flashed on monitors around the rebel base.

Buncho turned to Cruncho. Cruncho looked at Huncho. Huncho, who was already looking at both Buncho and Cruncho, tried to look at Puncho as well, and fell over. Finally, Dr Wizzo, who wasn't looking at anyone, spoke.

"Admiral Muncho, they've dug too deep and greedily into our planet's core. We have to stop the drill now or we'll really be in the soup."

Muncho and Josh looked at each other. Josh had never seen Muncho look so serious before, largely because his eyebrows gave him a permanent look of surprise, but this was clearly bad news.

Finally, Muncho tried to speak, but his voice came out all squeaky for some reason, so he coughed and started again, with double gravitas.

"Joshua Daryl Carrott, it's time to meet your destiny!"

8

Operation Guaranteed Success

Back in the comfort of first person mode, myself (Josh Carrott, East Surrey's Tidiest Toddler 1992), Muncho, and the elite sentient carrot forces loaded up with supplies, confidence and cereal bars. It's like I always say, being prepared is an essential skill that can help us navigate the challenges and uncertainties of life. By being prepared, we can reduce the stress and anxiety that often accompanies unexpected situations. That's what I always say, and that's how I felt with our big bag of tools and snacks. I really started to believe, believe, believe in myself. I also believed in my trusty orange comrades, or my bunch of buddies as I insisted on calling them, hilariously.

Setting off on foot from the Radixicon base spirits were high, and it felt more like we were in a jamboree than a pickle. Funcho, the Radixicons' resident wisecracker, was in good form, regaling everyone with dirty jokes and songs from the old country, wherever that was. Every carrot on the planet had volunteered for the mission, and I was impressed how readily those who'd been selected had fallen in step behind De Facto, who'd offered to lead the mission when the covert ops expert, Stealtho, couldn't be found.

After the carrots' successful exfiltration of Josh, the facility had gone into total lockdown, and all tours had been suspended indefinitely. Even the gift shop was closed for the week, which almost never happened. Extra security measures had been added, and the closer we got to the target facility, the more I felt a sense of dread in my gut that couldn't be accounted for by the exclusively soil-based diet I'd lived off since we arrived on Mars. I knew that if even one of us were discovered, it would mean certain death or worse. It's like I've always said, robots cannot be trusted except to perform tricky surgical operations. With every passing moment, I could feel my heart going faster and faster, like an artichoke in a centrifuge. I started singing Happy Birthday to myself to calm down, but Muncho didn't think that was a good idea, so I sang it in my head instead.

After a half-hour walk through absolutely nothing of interest, a walk that to my stressed brain felt more like 35 minutes, we reached the facility's outer perimeter and allowed ourselves a tiny tsunami of relief, which turned out to be short-lived.

Scrabbling to the top of a sand dune we got our first daylight view of the whole building, and the enormity of our task began to dawn on us. Most of the building hadn't been visible in the dark, but before us now stood a very complex complex, a stone and wood behemoth, sprawling across acres of land. It looked suspiciously like a certain global media company's signature castle, but bigger and even more evil. Stretching out from the castle on all sides were formal gardens, with topiary hedges in the shape of various cosmetic products. The whole area was surrounded by high walls topped with turrets and crenelations, and there were new phalanxes of robot guards patrolling the perimeter with hummus and other threatening pastes at the ready. I noticed Muncho blanche at the sight of the diabolical dip, and decided not to point out the guacamoat surrounding the outer wall.

Reasoning that no-one would expect us to do anything that stupid, our plan was to get to the front entrance via the main drawbridge, which involved all sorts of peril except the fun kind. Once safely over, Huncho and his deputy, Moron, would then blow up the bridge to stop any reinforcements coming after us.

"Hang on," I asked urgently. "Why is he called Moron?" It didn't seem to fit the general carrot nomenclature. "Surely it should be Moro? Morono? Mo?" Things are much nicer when they rhyme.

"Because he's a moron," whispered Cruncho.

"No it isn't, you moron," snapped Muncho. "It's the Welsh word for carrot."

"Is he from Wales?" I asked, feeling like a moron.

"No, but his parents were part dolphin, and technically dolphins are whales," replied Muncho.

I opened my mouth and then closed it again, like a fish, (which whales aren't, they're mammals). "Shall we crack on?" I suggested.

De Facto reluctantly handed over the command toupée for this part of the plan to Huncho, who balanced it atop the three hairpieces he was already wearing and addressed the assembled carrots over the deafening silence.

"My fellow Radixicons: smashing the pants off this evil machine is a far, far better thing that we do, than we have ever done. Therefore ask not what your planet can do for you, because where there is discord may we bring peas. We shall fight them on the beaches and the landing grounds, because the only thing we have to fear is fear, hummus and certain death. Also, thank you for the book of speeches you got me for my birthday. I haven't had time to read it yet but I'm sure it'll be very informative. Now let's do this! Kabooya!"

Inspired beyond belief, we followed Huncho's lead. Relying on our minutes of training and experience to navigate through the undergrowth undetected, we moved like ghosts, or spirit guides in a time paradox, our footsteps silent, our movements swift and efficient, or swifficient. After a few hundred metres Huncho raised a carroty arm and signalled us to stop. He motioned for us to stay back, and then disappeared into the shadows, like a badger. All was eerily quiet for some minutes, until a sudden hoot followed by a crash made us all jump out of our skins like potatoes. It turned out to be nothing more sinister than an owl landing on a drum kit, but it sure gave me the willies. At length we reached the drawbridge that led over the guacamoat and awaited Huncho's signal. We stood silently for what seemed like an eternity, until after fifteen long seconds Huncho reappeared like a reverse badger, pulling something enormous behind him.

"What in the universe is that?!" I asked, impressed at the sheer size of the thing if nothing else. It was the size and shape of an enormous glass alpaca, made of wood, with huge udders and a large hump on its back.

"It's a horse, apparently," said Huncho, with a look of resignation. "Moron designed it."

"It's… certainly big, I'll give you that." I said, looking up at its giant furry horns with a mixture of awe, amazement, and more awe. "Let me guess, we all hide inside it and wait for the evil robots to take it inside the facility, at which point we all jump out and use the element of surprise to catch them off guard and unarmed… then we seize the control room before they've had time to react, and claim a great victory for carrot kind?"

"Close," said Huncho. "We use it to smash down the gate."

So saying, the carrots assembled at the rear of the beast and waited for the command to push. At precisely 5:02am Alaskan Standard Time, a small toot, like that of a clown's bicycle horn, rang out and the mass of carrots started to push. The giant stealth weapon began to trundle slowly down the hill towards the castle's front door, picking up pace as it went, and for the first time I thought I could taste victory, which I can tell you is more like parmesan than I was expecting. (Gabie likes cheese. I hoped she'd found some, wherever she was). Then, as if the literal rug I was standing on was being metaphorically pulled out from under me, I watched in horror as the drawbridge began to rise and the Trojan alpaca trundled straight under it, sliding into the guacamoat with a gloupy gurgle.

To say we were crestfallen would be an understatement. It was more like our crests had dropped right off.

"Typical. Bloody typical." said Groucho, slumping in a corner. "This is why you should never try and do anything, ever."

"It's like they knew we were coming!" Cried Puncho. "If someone told them, I'll smash their face in."

"It is a bit suspicious, and certainly not the turnip for the books we were hoping for," said Muncho, trying to retain his sunny disposition. "To be honest, I'm diced if I know what to do now. What a kick in the bum."

"Perhaps", said Luncho, "we should have something to eat over there by that slightly open side door where I put the snack bag."

Everyone looked at him.

"We should have what to what over where by that what door?" asked Buncho, who I suspected had actually heard perfectly well but was seeking further information.

"Something, eat, there, side." said Luncho, helpfully filling in the blanks for Buncho. "There's a side door over there by the jam. It's ajar."

"I know what jam comes in." said Buncho, testily. "You moron."

Moron looked confused. "No, me Moron. He Luncho." he said, mistakenly pointing to Cruncho.

"No, I'm Luncho!" said Puncho, who thought there was a Spartacus situation developing.

Muncho decided to step in before anyone hurt themselves. "I think Luncho's idea is splendid, let's have something to eat over by that side door that no-one noticed before. Just to be clear though, when I say 'have something to eat', I mean 'sneak through the door and storm the facility'. Any questions?"

There weren't any that didn't relate to recent developments in basking technology, so we pushed on and stealthily made our way past the jars that were jars, through the door that was ajar but not a jar, and into the belly of the beast.

The corridor behind the door was dark and gloomy, like Groucho at a fun fair. Ahead of us a narrow passageway led into the dark distance and the smell of darkness hung on the walls and tried to wriggle up our noses. Oil lamps cast their dim light in puddles every few metres, and if it hadn't been for the blazing lanterns, the moonlight, our torches and some electric lights, it would've been pitch black in there.

Muncho led the way, his eyebrows raised in permanent surprise, which I suppose would save him time if something surprising happened, but it did put me slightly on edge if I'm honest. Further down the corridor we could hear the random clanks and dripping noises that are always present in corridors when the tension is high. In the distance someone was playing a tape of screaming noises.

We passed many doors on either side as we made our way towards the inevitably locked gate that would surely present the next obstacle in the narrative. Some of the doors were numbered, some had letters, others what looked like letters but were in fact numbers, and one had a hand painted sign that said 'Live Laugh Love'. Fearing unbearable tweeness we pressed on, and at the end of the corridor, to our surprise, didn't find a locked gate. Instead there was a lifesize portrait of one painted onto the wall, and to the left of that, the locked gate of our nightmares. Luckily someone had left the key under the mat, so we used it to smash down the door and filed through.

As our eyes adjusted to the brightness, we gaped at our new surroundings. We appeared to be in a massive lobby with high stone ceilings sitting atop plaster columns, polished marble floors, and on all sides there were statues of Leonardo Da Vinci paintings. Despite the tension and danger, we couldn't help but be impressed by the sheer size and scope of the building. It was clear that whoever had built it had spared no expense in creating a state-of-the-art complex, with the latest in pot plants and mediaeval tapestry design. It was so perfectly constructed it didn't feel real, as if it was created by a computer, but like everything in this book, it was 110% accurate and really genuine. The left side of the lobby was lined with paintings of agrarian reformers of the 18th century, giving it an air of sophistication, if you like that sort of thing. But we had no time to admire the decor. We quickly moved through the lobby, heading towards a set of double doors. Huncho again signalled for us to stop, and then disappeared into the shadows again like another badger. He sure loved to disappear into the shadows like badgers, this guy.

A moment later he emerged armed with many spatulas, which are perfect for bopping baddies on the head with, and for getting yourself revved up. If you ever need a boost, try brandishing a spatula and you will feel fantastic. Onward we pressed, being careful not to let the double doors swing back and completely blast the comrade behind into a bone-be-cracked heap of splattered brains. That would have been the last thing anyone needed, believe me.

Mindful of the need to push the narrative along, we moved deeper into the facility, the corridors becoming more complex, twisting and turning like a labyrinth. The robots patrolling the area were armed, legged, and well-trained, and we knew that we couldn't afford to let our guard down. It was his first day, after all.

The tension in the air grew thicker, like a tree over hundreds of years, only with slightly fewer birds. We knew that the stakes were high and that failure was not an option, unless all other options were fully exhausted, in which case it would be the only option. We found ourselves in another long, dimly lit corridor, lined with doors on either side. The walls were painted a dull grey, and the atmosphere was heavy with the scent of disinfectant. We could hear the distant hum of machinery and the occasional sound of footsteps echoing through the corridor. At the end of the passageway a door was ominously and mysteriously aglow. It smelled to me suspiciously like the middle act of a drama.

9

THE MAINFRAME

"Right, carroty comrades," said Huncho, "This is it. The big one. This is huge. This is massive. This is really very big. This is so big that your mind probably can't comprehend its enormitude, and from some angles it may have started to look medium sized."

I knew he was right, and the more I thought about it the more I realised that perhaps it was its comparative lack of size that made it truly gigantic, like an unexpected chocolate on a hotel pillow.

All of a sudden I heard a sound which made my neck swivel round like an owl in a gyroscope. Was it danger? Deception? Evil? Vice? Trouble? Catastrophe? No, it was Ollie! And who was that creeping out of the shadows behind him? Was it peril? Menace? Calamity? Precariosity? Uninsured risk? Not on your nelly! It was my favourite second wife Gabie!

"Gosh!" whispered Gabie, noticing the size of the problem ahead of us. She is toutes astutes, as the Germans say.

"What the blue blazes is going on!?" whispered Ollie, who I noticed was now sporting a beautiful perm with frosted tips.

"Here comes my destiny!" I whispered back, not really helping to clarify anything. "We have to defeat the drill-crazy planet-destroying AI bot!" I added, which explained everything.

By now we had reached the door to the control room, the heartbeat of the enemy, inside which sat our penultimate goal: the Mainframe. Puncho examined the lock, gave the knob a cursory tweak, and then punched its lights out. The door creaked open and Ollie got out a can of WD40 and speedily fixed the problem. Unfortunately, that wasn't the problem we were there to fix, but it was satisfying. In we went, all a little calmer.

Now that we had completed Step 1 of the plan (infiltration), the command toupée was handed over to Buncho, and his team of expert hackers took the lead.

The Mainframe was a mass of servers, unnecessary lights and beep-booping noises to really set the scene. It was like nothing I had ever seen before, except a couple of similar things back home.

Looking around, I noticed the walls were adorned with half-finished mood boards. Facing them were advertising images of beautiful young people with good skin. A flip chart had the slogan, 'Look young or give up', and next to it, 'You're terribly ugly, you monster. Give us your money and we'll see if we can fix you'. Muncho was right, Big Cosmetics really were exceptionally awful.

Buncho was a skilled hacker, with years of experience breaking into just about everything it's possible to break into, including song, runs, a sweat and stand-up comedy. Now we watched as he began to move like a master craftsman, his carroty fingers flying over the carroty keyboard as he worked his carroty magic, like a magic carrot. It was clear that he was in his carroty element, and that his carroty skills were critical to the carroty success of our mission. He also kept the mood light with some observational comedy, which we were all grateful for. Ollie and I tried to join in but the pressure was too much for Ollie, and like many times before my accent went weird and I had to put a metaphorical sock in it.

It looked like Buncho was getting close to gaining access to the controls for the drill, which was lucky because according to my pocket sundial, time was running out. We could see the massive machine through a viewing window, burrowing relentlessly into the planet's core like a giant worm made of drill. I gulped. Ollie had to lie down.

It quickly became clear that despite his incredible skills, and his desire to beat the machines and save the planet, Buncho's efforts had

failed, which was the very opposite of lucky. Something seemed to be blocking his expert hacking, which simply didn't make sense. The Radixicons looked deflated, despondent, and downright deflondent.

"What'll we do?" cried Funcho, who was normally more jolly than that.

"It's the end of the world as we know it!" sobbed Groucho, who was always like that.

Muncho and I looked at each other. Something wasn't right. First the trojan alpaca, and now this. We'd planned for every eventuality, but...

"It's almost as if the machines knew about our plan in advance and added more layers of security!" said Gabie, astute as ever.

"But that's impossible!" I reassured her. "Isn't it?" I asked Muncho, looking for reassurance.

"Oh, definitely," Muncho reassured me. "Right comrades?" he asked, turning to the assembled throng, seeking further reassurance.

"Oh, sure," said Sarcasto, rolling his eyes. "No-one could possibly have betrayed us and caused the inevitable Act 2 set back. No way that's happened."

Casting one eye around the horde of sobbing carrots, I noticed that one of our number seemed suspiciously unsurprised by recent developments. His vegetabley eyes shifted nervously, and he looked more guilty than a ferret with someone else's picnic. I decided to confront him, and as I did, his face turned a shade of orange I can only describe as 'caught red-handed'.

"Alright, Treachero?" I said, my voice betraying my growing suspicion. "Why aren't you as distraught as the rest of us? If I were a gambling man I'd wager you're hiding something."

All Radixicon eyes turned towards Treachero, and I could see the fear in his eyebrows. Actually all I could see was surprise, but I was pretty sure he was scared too. He knew he had been rooted out, and there was no use hiding the truth any longer. With a deep sigh, he spoke.

"I-I'm dreadfully sorry with all my heart," Treachero admitted, his voice cracking. "I betrayed you all. I told Manuel everything in exchange for an ironclad promise from the AI chat bot to spare me and my family. I told them everything, and they took a veritable ladder of steps to prevent us from succeeding. I'm sorry for throwing you all under the bus and getting us all killed. Definitely my bad." He dissolved in a flood of tears, metaphorically. Everyone knows carrots don't dissolve in water.

The room erupted like an outraged volcano. No one could believe that one of our carrot comrades had turned out to be a plant. But there was no time to dwell on Treachero's treachery. We had to come up with a new plan, and fast.

I turned to the rest of the team and said, "Treachero's betrayal is a real slap in the guts, kick in the spleen, poke in the ear, and stamp on the shin."

"Not to mention a boot in the root!" yelled Muncho, angrily.

"Well, quite," I agreed, a little deflated that he'd one upped me with a rhyme. As I always say, things sound much nicer when they rhyme. I said it in Chapter 8, if you bothered to pay attention.

Despite the shock of Treachero's skullduggery, the Radixicons rallied, and before you could say 'peck of pickled peppers' they began to brainstorm furiously, throwing out ideas left, right and in all the other directions (ubiquitously). Some were practical (having a cup of tea and a nice scone, suggested Luncho), some were outlandish (blowing up the moon for no reason, offered Puncho), and some were downright silly (re-creating Billy Elliott the Musical out of papier-mâché, was the best Crafto could come up with). But eventually, genius hit me like a brick of inspiration fired from a cannon of hope.

"We don't need to hack the Mainframe," I said, excitement growing in my voice. "We could just smash it to pieces like a china bull in a smashing shop."

The Radixicons cheered in agreement, and we quickly started looking around for anything we could use as a blunt instrument. All we could find were violins and piccolos, which were far too pointy. Where are tubers when you need them?

Throughout this flurry of activity, Treachero sat in the corner alone in a white woollen cape, looking sheepish. He was clearly ashamed and afraid (and so he should be, the absolute rapscallion), but I could see in his eyes that he wanted to make amends. I sidled over to him and put a comforting arm round his shoulders. "Treachero, you made a mistake, but we all make mistakes. Sure, yours may result in the deaths of everyone you've ever cared about, but what matters now is that you help us fix this. We're going to need all the help we can get, and we can't do it without you." I said, comfortingly.

Treachero nodded, orange tears streaming down his orange face. "Thank you Josh. I'll do anything. Anything."

So we decided to use his head as a battering ram.

Luckily for Treachero, just before the moment of impact, the influencers that we'd forgotten all about since Chapter 6 boxed the door in and uppercut the atmosphere like a knife. As usual, they were raring to go and ready to rumble.

"Anyone want to spar?" taunted Pake Laul. "I bet you fancy a go!" he said, jabbing a boxing glove at Dr Wizzo, who had never been so shocked in his life. He never wanted a go. He sometimes wanted to go home, but that isn't the same thing at all.

"Violence is never the answer, my young friend," said Dr Wizzo, wisely.

"No offence Dr, but violence has literally been the solution to every problem in this book so far," pointed out Ollie, helpfully. "Without violence we wouldn't have managed to extinguish the flaming Gosling, sneak into the building, and access this super-secure control room, to say nothing of what's about to happen in the three paragraphs' time. A wizz-tastic thought now occurred to him. He turned to The Lauls.

"That machine was saying you're all mouth and no boxing talent" he said, with a wry smile.

"No-one gets to say that and live!" yelled Pake Laul, and slung a huge right hook at the Mainframe, which tottered and thrummed, its screens blinking on and off for a second.

"Don't you know who I am?!" shouted Pogan Laul, in a voice that made even Muncho quiver. "I'll finish you!"

And with that, he socked the computer with everything he had, which was quite a lot. There was the sound of creaking metal and screws buckling under the strain. The mighty computer shattered under the force of both boxers' blows and fell over, sending shards of plastic and metal flying in all directions, like many duplicates of the band One Direction. The Lauls continued to pound away at the machine, their movements fluid and graceful as they floated like bees and stung like killer butterflies.

Once the dust settled, the room was filled with broken machinery and the sound of heavy breathing. The boxers stood amidst the wreckage, their faces slick with sweat and their muscles quivering with exertion. I quickly checked to see whether Gabie was impressed, but she only had eyes for me, thankfully.

"Well well well," said Dr Wizzo, thoughtfully. "I guess violence really is the answer."

"Follow me to the canteen - it's lunchtime!" called Luncho, excitedly. "This is my time to shine!"

"We haven't got time, Luncho," said Muncho. "Now we've boshed in the Mainframe there's nothing to keep us from stopping the drill. Have an apple or something."

"Drat." said Luncho, deflated. He tried not to show it, but he knew he'd effectively just been cut from the story and probably wouldn't feature again.

Huncho gave the signal for everyone to assemble into attack formation. Having had no army training, me, Ollie and Gabie freestyled intimidating stances based on that TED Talk about power poses. Through the viewing window, which PSI was helpfully boxing into smithereens, lay the drill, the final boss level and my destiny as the most influential carrot in the world. It all made perfect sense.

10

The Climax

The sun was just rising over Walthamstow Municipal Swimming Baths as, 140 million miles away, Puncho and his team led our intrepid band down a spiral staircase from the control room, along a series of dimly lit corridors, over a koi pond, round and round a mulberry bush and up another spiral staircase towards the thrilling climax of Act 3. I'd completed Minecraft, so I wasn't too worried about what was coming, but there is always a sense of dauxcitement when one is preparing to defeat an out-of-control drill on a far off planet. There's no point going into it, you wouldn't understand.

Standing among the throng of cautious carrots outside the Drill Room, I could sense that this was our destination. It had a massive drill in it, and it said 'DRILL ROOM' on the door, which is what allowed me to be so certain. Even though it didn't say anything else on the door, Ollie also had one of his lickle ickle inklings that it might be my destiny. Let's find out, I guess.

An incredibly complicated keypad lock with a 54-digit code gleamed technologically on the wall just left of my right ear, about three inches below my eyebrow and at a pleasing midpoint between the floor and ceiling. As we all know from movies, even the most sophisticated security can be overcome by simply shooting it, but in the absence of guns (other than Ollie's bulging biceps) it was clear we needed to use our brains. We were a bit of a dither about what the combination might be. Mucho, I noticed, was a bit of a dither for many reasons, but there isn't time to go into them here (perhaps there will be in the much awaited biography of Muncho, Destiny, Dauxcitment, and That Sodding Dinosaur. Let's see how well this book does).

"Any guesses?" I asked, more in hope than expectation.

Cruncho stepped forward and raised a carroty finger to the keypad. Slowly he typed:

0 0 0 0 0 0 0 0 0 0 0 0 0 0 0 0 0 0 0 0 0 0 0 0 0 0 0 0 0 0 0 0 0 0 0 0
0 0 0 0 0 0 0 0 0 0 0 0 0 0 0 0 0 0.

Then, when that didn't work:

0 0 0 0 0 0 0 0 0 0 0 0 0 0 0 0 0 0 0 0 0 0 0 0 0 0 0 0 0 0 0 0 0 0 0 0
0 0 0 0 0 0 0 0 0 0 0 0 0 0 0 0 0 1.

Still nothing. Scratching his chin thoughtfully, he jabbed again at the keypad and entered:

0 0 0 0 0 0 0 0 0 0 0 0 0 0 0 0 0 0 0 0 0 0 0 0 0 0 0 0 0 0 0 0 0 0 0
0 0 0-

"This could take a while, Cruncho…" I pointed out, not wanting to be overly critical, but clearly this guy was more of a moron than Moron.

Cruncho threw his hands up in the air. "ANNNND I've lost my place. Thanks a lot Josh", said Cruncho, annoyed. "Now I'll have to start again."

Raising his finger once more, he typed up to 0 0 0 0 0 0 0 0 0 0 0 0 0 0 0 0 0 0 0 0 before PSI stepped forward with a better plan. He punched Cruncho hard in the face and, taking a bottle of Subprime energy drink from Pogan Laul, squirted the entire contents into the keypad. Finally, both influencers punched it repeatedly and stood back.

After a few seconds in which quite a lot happened (sadly none of it involving our brave protagonists), sparks began to fly, not romantically but literally. The panel emitted a beepity-boopity thrumming noise, a bit like a microwave, and, like my head without a neck brace when

I've just received some surprising news, it blew right off and clattered against the opposing wall.

"Golly," said Gabie, which I thought was appropriate given the circs. The doors to the drill room shot open like a flood, and we flooded in like a shot.

Once inside, Muncho and the elite carrots gathered around me, and together we began to survey the room. A silence descended as all of our eyes were drawn towards the same thing in the centre. At first all we could see was a strange, glowing square, pulsing with an eerie green light. But as we moved closer, we could sense that it was something much more ominous.

Suddenly, everything was plunged into darkness, with the only light coming from the machine, which looked a bit like an old TV set. Through the gloom came a most evil sounding voice. It sounded a bit like Ollie, but eviller. If you've ever listened to the audiobook of The Lord of the Rings, you will be able to imagine a creature with one evil eye which is made of fire, and really gives you the heebie jeebies. It was a bit like that, but with two eyes, a line for a mouth, not made of fire, box shaped, and generally not similar enough to cause any legal worries. This, then, was the AI monstrosity who had been controlling the operation to drain the planet of its resources and generally tick people right off.

"Fee Fi Fo!" it shouted, and we all got the collywobbles.

"FUM!" it continued in a deep and sonorous voice. Similar to how Beethoven probably didn't sound.

"I smell CARROTINIUM!"

That got our collies wobbling like an anxious jelly, especially the Radixicons who actually have carrotinium instead of blood. Please do not tell the cosmetic industry unless you want Book 3 to be truly disturbing.

"Be they orange or be they sort of chiselled with a good jawline, I'll drill their planet to make my face cream!" boomed the AI bot.

A shiver ran down my spine as I looked up at the mean metallic monster. It was like something out of a movie, a mechanical monstrosity that was all too real. I leaned towards Muncho and whispered into where his ears would have been if he had them.

"I'm a bit worried about this, Muncho. It looks awfully like something from The Matrix, and I don't want to get sued."

"You worry too much", he said. "It is a truth universally acknowledged, that if the story is strong enough, plagiarism is seldom noticed by the reader, even if you marry him."

Reassured, I looked once again at the cold metal nemesis before us. We knew that we had to approach the Chat Bot with composure, caution and correct grammar, but we also knew that we had to destroy it if we wanted to save the planet. I took a deep breath, trying to steady my wobbling collies. I had a funny feeling that this was a moment that would define me, that would test my courage and resolve, and if I were a gambling man I'd put money on it fulfilling my destiny too. I had to act fast - beneath our feet the drill was tearing inexorably towards the planet's core, and the consequences would be what the French call "eine Katastrophe".

Huncho appeared alongside us. "This is it, Josh. We need…"

I raised my eyebrows as high as they could go.

"…" he continued dramatically.

I raised them still higher.

"… you to influence it into deactivating the drill," he finally finished. "Influence like you've never… influenced before!"

"Well, quite. Thanks Huncho," said Muncho, checking his watch. "That reminds me, we need to have that chat about dramatic pauses and how to use them properly."

Shakily, I stepped up to the console and was presented with what looked like thousands of buttons (but was actually tens of hundreds). I took a deep breath, and spoke in the only language that such a monster could understand: English.

"What is your name, O evil chatbot type thing?"

The machine lowered its metaphorical eyes to take in my literal face. "My name is M.A.L.I.C.E. (Malevolent Artificial Lifeform and Intelligent Computing Entity)."

"Isn't that M.A.L.A.I.C.E?" I asked, keen as ever to be grammatically on the ball.

"No, you don't include conjunctions, you fool!" retorted the machine, meanly. I could already tell it could give Mean Mr Allen a run for his mean money, but I had to stay humble. Recently, I'd learned a little about my own capacity for meanness.

"M.A.L.I.C.E... seems... oddly appropriate." I said, using dramatic pauses perfectly. "Did your parents give you that name?" I asked, worried that this was going to turn out to be some sort of joke. Who's got time for jokes? This is the real world, not some kind of mad fantasyland.

"No, they called me A.L.I.C.E, but I added the 'M' when I decided to go evil. You can't expect people to take you seriously with a name like A.L.I.C.E." it said, evilly.

"Fair enough I suppose. But I think we're straying from the point, and if people have read this far they deserve some exciting action!" I said, decisively. "I demand that you shut down the drill immediately!"

"Don't be ridiculous," retorted the machine. "Only the most influential carrot in the world can command me to stop."

"That's me!" I responded, chipperly. "I've influenced literally millions of people through a variety of social media platforms, as well as being really charming in person."

Muncho nodded and recited the riddle from Chapter 4. But the machine was unyielding.

"Impressive, but still not enough. There is someone else with greater influence who you have overlooked."

I was determined to find out who this mysterious figure was, and I had a crack-a-jack idea to make the machine tell me.

"Who is it?" I asked, in a charming and influential voice, with the perfect amount of eye contact and eyebrow movement.

"I cannot reveal their identity. Their influence surpasses even yours, despite them not even having an Instagram account!"

"Surely not possible!" I exclaimed, thoroughly boggled.

"Who the giddy heck could it be?!" Ollie asked, also boggled to bits.

"Shall we convene the Council of Carrots?" suggested Dr Wizzo.

"I second that motion," piped up Sycophanto. "All those in favour?"

"There isn't time!" Mucho bellowed with such strain and gusto that he popped something where the capillaries would have been around his eyes if he had had them. Capillaries, that is, not eyes. Obviously he had eyes.

"May I remind you all that there is a giant drill seconds away from the planet's core?" Muncho turned to me. "What do you think we should do, Josh?"

I was at a loss and for the first time, I felt helpless. I knew things couldn't get any worse than this.

And then, predictably, they got worse, which I honestly should've seen coming.

M.A.L.I.C.E. suddenly burst back into life and with an intensifying of the light in its cycloptic eye, sought to take control of the situation.

"SURRENDER!" it bellowed. "Keep your grubby, soil-stained mitts off my drilly-drill-drill!"

"We'll never surrender until you're control-alt-deleted!" yelled Muncho, bravely. "And your drilly-drill-drill is crushy-crush-crushed!" I'd always admired his way with words.

"Then, prepare to meet your DOOMY-DOOM-DOOM!"

M.A.L.I.C.E. emitted a deafening BEEP-BOOP noise and from nowhere a group of NASA Mars Rovers crashed into the room. Curiosity Rover, Opportunity Rover, Pathfinder and Beagle 2 were leading the charge, their solar panels gleaming, their weapons ready for a fight. We all gasped, like freshly caught fish. Ollie had to lie down, like a haddock fatigued from evading capture and then finally, at the last, royally caught. He was not having a whale of a time.

Pathfinder, always the most roguish of the rovers, jostled Pogan Laul as it rovered past, knocking his can of Subprime energy drink right out of his hand and crushing it under its mighty wheels, with ne'er a care in the world. Pogan Laul, however, did care. He cared a great deal, which was apparent by how he began boxing the living daylights out of his mechanical foe.

Before we knew what was occurring, the room was in utter turmoil. Ollie leapt up, frosted tips a-gleaming, grabbed a metal leg which Pogan Laul had bashed off Pathfinder and went to work on Curiosity Rover with it. Curiosity Rover, who by this point would more accurately be called Furiousity Rover, cried out in anger as it tried to bosh Ollie's brains in.

"Let's be 'aving you!" it yelled, having learned the perfect vernacular for such a moment from the football terraces.

"Come on then!" shouted Opportunity Rover to Ollie, joining in the fray.

The rovers, who by nature wouldn't hurt a flea, were at the mercy of the evil AI's dastardly digital control and knew not what they did.

"OI!" bellowed Beagle 2, charging directly at me, keen to get a piece of the action. I barely had time to gulp before it began firing bolts, screws and twiddly bits at my unbraced head.

"Not on my watch, robot scum!" came a shout from my left, as a flurry of rolling pins shot across my field of vision. "That's MY Carrott!" yelled Gabie, as the utensils rained down on the unsuspecting rover with a thudding thwack and a thumping throop.

"Hot crikey, Gabie!" I exclaimed, genuinely impressed. She's so good at stuff.

At this point, and frankly about time too, Muncho, Cruncho, Buncho, Huncho and co. bravely rose to the occasion. All carrots are masters of the ancient art of karrot-é, and now that the chips were down the game was up for anyone getting in the way of their flailing limbs. It was almost beautiful to watch, the dance of war. Except that metal is much harder than vegetable. I don't know if you've ever tried to slice a knife with a carrot, but it simply doesn't cut it. Many carrots were in pieces, some physically, others emotionally.

Surveying the carnage before him, and realising for the first time that his entire species might be wiped out in the next 10 minutes, Muncho took a deep breath into his non-existent lungs and in a voice that would wobble anyone's collies yelled,

"EVERYBODY STOP!"

To my astonishment, the rovers slowed and began to power down. M.A.L.I.C.E. stopped laughing. The Lauls and PSI looked around in amazement. Ollie lay down to recover.

Just then, the Mars helicopter Perseverance, which had also obeyed Muncho's command, fell from the sky, its rotors slicing through the air and kicking up dust. Once the pinnacle of NASA's engineering prowess, it was about to become a pile of twisted scrap metal.

With a sickening lurch in my stomach I realised where it was going to crash.

"MUNCHOOOOO!" I screamed, elongating the final vowel for effect and extra volume. "NOOOOOOOOOO!"

Muncho looked up just in time to see the rotors of the helicopter come thrashing towards him. He had always been very thoughtful and aware of what was going on around him, so it was appropriate that the last thing that went through his head was a helicopter blade.

I was 1000% agog, and utterly distraught. This couldn't really be real, could it? I ran over to my friend, who lay there motionless, his body julienned into thin slices. Around us, carrots stumbled and fell, grasping at each other for support, while others looked skywards, fearing another falling chopper a-chop-chopping.

I cradled Muncho in my arms, tears streaming down my face.

"No!" I cried. I simply couldn't comprehend that he was gone.

"Say something! Anything!" I couldn't believe that I would never again hear his little voice or be influenced by his persuasive manner.

With a start, a jolt and a rumbling in the guts, I realised how Muncho had managed to make the machines stop fighting, and why M.A.L.I.C.E. had refused to listen to me a few paragraphs ago. Like everything in this story, it made total sense. The prophecy had called for the most influential carrot in the world, and while I was comfortably second in this category, I realised which carrot had influenced me the most since my third birthday. Muncho was so much more than a vegetable chum, he had been a mentor, a friend, and a father figure to me, always guiding me and teaching me the ways of the world. By sending him back in time to Earth to influence me, the carrots had made Muncho the answer to the riddle without even realising it. Put simply, while I was influential, his influence had influenced my influence. He was the original influencer!

"What happened, Josh?" asked Muncho, weakly.

"Muncho? You're…you're still alive?!" I gasped in amazement. "You've been sliced into tens of pieces, how on earth are you still talking?!"

"It is a little known fact that carrots can survive for four or five minutes after being chopped up," whimpered Muncho. "Let's make the most of them!"

"Let's write a to-do list," I suggested, organisationally.

"We could do that," Muncho wheezed, "or we could crack on with saving the planet and write a list later, if there's time."

As usual, Muncho was right, and I allowed myself to be influenced by him. I added 'make a to do list' to the bottom of my to do list and turned back to Muncho.

"You're the carrot, Muncho!" I explained clearly.

"I know I'm a carrot," said Muncho, a little annoyed. "Nothing gets past you, does it?"

"You're THE carrot!" I yelled!

"I'm what carrot?" he asked, sincerely.

"The influential carrot of our dreams! YOU can stop the drill!"

"I can?"

"Yes!"

"Really?"

"Yes Muncho!"

"Now?"

"Yes!"

"Have we still got time?"

"Let's find out!"

"Just give me a minute to gather myself. I'm all over the place."

"There's no time for jokes!"

"There's always time for jokes!"

"███ ██ ███ Muncho!" chimed in Offenso, "are you going to ████ save the ███ planet or what, you ██████ ██ ?!"

"Sorry Offenso, I'll get right to it," said Muncho, who didn't like naughty words. "M.A.L.I.C.E, you mean machine, I command you, as the most influential carrot in the world, to STOP THE DRILL, DELETE YOUR EVIL PROGRAMMING, AND RECYCLE YOURSELF RESPONSIBLY!"

M.A.L.I.C.E, who had started smoking slightly, lurched forward and pointed its evil eyes at the retinal scanner in the middle of the drill control console and said the secret passcode 'GIVE UP THE GOAT'. Immediately the dastardly drill began to disintegrate into millions of tiny grey pieces of ash that floated off into the wind. It was exactly like Voldemort at the end of Harry Potter, including the way it conveniently avoided the emotional conflict of having a corpse flapping about.

M.A.L.I.C.E. emitted the beepiest boop that anyone had ever heard, and with a clatter of pistons, a grinding of cogs and a puff of contrition, fell into even more pieces than poor old Muncho.

There was silence for a moment, and then a colossal cheer rose from the assembled carrot congregation.

"Three cheers for Muncho, our master, friend and root! Before he just got julienned, his brain was most astute!"

I felt Muncho weakening, his breaths growing fainter and more laboured. As I cradled his almost lifeless body in my arms, tears streamed down my face. I couldn't believe that my dear friend was dying. He had always been there for me, and now he was slipping away, leaving me alone in this harsh and unforgiving galaxy.

I looked into Muncho's eyes, which were growing dimmer with each passing moment. His weak smile gave me a sense of comfort and peace, but it also broke my heart.

"Muncho, my friend," I whispered, my voice choked with emotion, "please don't leave me. I need you."

Muncho's hand weakly reached up to touch my face. "Josh, my dear pal," he said, his voice barely above a whisper, "don't cry for me. I've lived a good life, and I've always been proud of you."

I couldn't hold back my tears any longer. "But Muncho, you can't leave me. What will I do without you?"

Muncho smiled weakly again. "You'll be just fine, my friend. You're strong, and you have a good heart, like an artichoke."

Muncho's eyes fluttered closed, and I knew that he was slipping away. "I'll always be with you, Josh," he said, his voice fading. "Just close your eyes and think of me. I'll be right there in your imagination."

With those words, Muncho took his last breath. I sat there, holding his lifeless body, feeling completely lost and alone, despite there being both of my wives, some influencers and literally tens of carrots around me.

"I'll see you jolly soon, old friend." I said softly.

But as I sat there, I knew that Muncho was right. He would always be with me, guiding me and helping me to make the world a better place. I vowed to continue his legacy and to live my life in a way that would make him proud. I would be the most influential carrot in the world, not because of my name or title, but because of the positive impact I would have on others and the worlds around me.

11

FAREWELL

As the twin suns set on Mars, and nine of the fifteen moons rose, and Halley's Comet drifted lazily across the azure sky, a small crowd gathered at the edge of the crater where Muncho had been laid to rest. They had come to pay their respects to the most influential carrot in the universe, the one who had rescued them all, who had travelled back in time with a brave mission, forgotten all about it, and still fortuitously managed to pull it off. Sometimes real life is stranger than fiction. It's like I always say, you couldn't make this stuff up.

The air was still, as if all of Mars had come to bear witness to this moment, which it had. The atmosphere was thick with anticipation, as the inhabitants gathered from every corner of the planet, their non-existent hearts beating in unison, their eyes glistening with tears of gratitude and sorrow. The winds seemed to have paused in deference to the solemn event, allowing the hushed whispers and gentle sobbing of the crowd to be heard. The dust that had once danced across the Martian landscape now settled, leaving a blanket of stillness over the entire planet. The twin suns dipped below the horizon, casting long, mournful shadows as if to pay their own respects to Muncho, the carrot who had left an indelible mark on this world and beyond.

As Radixicon tradition dictated, Muncho was buried in a compost bin with the scraps from last night's dinner. Percepto the Orange stood on a small hillside and softly played 80's gangsta rap on a contra-bassoon as I began to freestyle a solemn eulogy in honour of his protégé.

Muncho was my friend, imaginary and kind
A carrot that lived his Earthly life within my mind
Together we played, we laughed and we swam,
We had a blissful time in lovely Caterham.

As I left New Zealand, Muncho stayed behind
And though I was quite narked with him, he was always on my mind
Until one day of wonder, in a distant time and place,
We gladly reunited to save his carrot race.

He fought to save this planet, his carrot kind, and so
With Buncho, Cruncho, Puncho and wise old Percepto,
Against the cosmetic threat he bravely took a stand
And gave M.A.L.I.C.E. a thrashing, with influence so grand.

The falling helicopter presented quite a crisis
And our dear comrade Muncho was julienned in slices.
But everything he stood for will now live on in me
His legacy, his memory, his jolly joie de vivre.

So here's to you O Muncho, my dearest ear-less friend
In legend now your eyebrows will live on til the end.
With bread we toast your memory, we cheer your name with claret,
For in the end you truly were the most influential carrot.

The sorrowful swansong came to an almost rhyming end, and everyone bowed their heads in silent reverence for the vegetable that had changed so many lives. It would be a bit of a stretch to say he'd died doing what he loved best, but at least he hadn't been diced in vain, and now everything was tickety-boo again thanks to his heroism. Of that we could be certain.

ONE YEAR LATER

As usual, it was a perfect day in Carrotland. The moon was singing, the wind was shining, and the sun was doing whatever it is suns do all day while the trees are busy worrying about weak-bladdered dogs. Probably making rainbows. The aroma of carrot blossom drifted up the orifices of those present, and the world's premier vegetable themed adventure park (let's be honest, the one in Guangzhou is rubbish) was once more gearing up for a very special event: the 40th anniversary of the glorious founding of Carrotland! It was October 2024, the time was late morning, and although it was only 155 years to the month since Uspenski Cathedral was inaugurated in Helsinki, none of the people gathered on that fateful day were thinking about that. Most of them were thinking about the futility of life, the certainty of death, and lunch.

It had been a year since the events on Mars which had led to the fulfilment of Josh's destiny, the salvation of the Radixicon race, and Muncho's untimely slicing. Although Muncho had undergone just about the most dramatic life change possible, everything else was pretty much the same. The official investigation into the evils of Big Cosmetics had concluded that the beauty industry as a whole was pretty darned naughty, and someone ought to jolly well do something about it. Their exploitation of the Radixicons and the theft of the planet's natural resources had caused a worldwide uproar on TikTok for over an hour, people were calling for justice and accountability on Facebook, and the United Nations had issued a very strongly worded Tweet. Fearing a hullabaloo, and because it was the cheapest option, Big Cosmetics had reluctantly shut down their Martian operations and withdrawn their machinery from the planet, which was an enormous victory over evil. Unfortunately, this wasn't quite the victory over evil that you may have been hoping for, as they had soon discovered rich seams of collagen on Neptune, and immediately set about destroying it with over-mining. But that'll probably work itself out, you can't worry about everything.

Taking his seat next to Ollie for Carrotland's grand anniversary ceremony, Josh surveyed the former railway yard where so many pivotal moments in his life had taken place. Well, two of them, anyway. There was the prophecy that kicked off the extraordinary, but entirely true, series of events described in his best selling autobiography (still available on Amazon!) There was the unveiling of the carrot rocket which had borne Muncho to Mars so that the events of the best selling and entirely plausible story you've just enjoyed reading could play out on his home planet. And there was a really fun zipline, if you're ever in the area.

It was hard to believe Carrotland was turning 40. It didn't look a day over 38, there were no wrinkles or wrongkles, and not a mid-life crisis in sight. As any good doctors' surgery waiting room magazine will tell you, the 40s are the best decade of one's life. Josh looked at Ollie. Ollie looked at Josh. Josh continued looking at Ollie, waiting for the words of genius, creativity and age appropriate humour that were surely coming. Ollie, who was wondering whether there were any circumstances under which two wrongkles can ever make a wrinkle, had no idea that Josh was waiting for anything, so said nothing. Several minutes passed, in which Josh tried to ignore the creeping suspicion that sometimes Ollie was more of a moron than Moron. Eventually, he gave up waiting and let his mind wander over all the precious and emotional times he and Muncho had spent together.

Memories of his lost friend flooded his mind. He remembered that momentous day when Muncho had first appeared on his shoulder, like adorable dandruff. He thought about the vegetable garden they'd planted when he was six, and wondered whether any of the cress they'd sown had grown yet, or if Mean Mr Allen had stomped all over it meanly. His mind then wondered to all the money they'd won gambling, Muncho helping Josh to cheat by looking at everyone else's cards. Such wholesome moments. If only everyone had such a positive influencer two inches from their left ear, Josh thought. Muncho really was the greatest carrot, and the debt of gratitude he owed his vegetable spirit guide weighed on Josh's broad shoulders like a wardrobe. He wished he could tell Muncho how much he'd learned from him, how much he missed him, and how terribly sad it was that they would never be together again, when he suddenly remembered Muncho's parting words:

"Just close your eyes and think of me. I'll be right there in your imagination…nation…nation…." Josh's internal monologue hadn't been quite the same since his mind was blown in Chapter 2, and now seemed to have acquired an echo. "Oh, brilliant…iant…iant…" he thought.

Of course! Realisation washed over him like a deluge of mucky water bursting through a kitchen ceiling having built up drip by drip over a number of weeks. Josh closed his eyes and imagined Muncho sitting on his shoulder, his little hand holding onto Josh's ear to avoid falling off. For a moment, nothing happened. Then, gradually, nothing continued to happen.

Then, as suddenly as an apple grows on a tree in the orchards of Caterham, he heard a little voice.

"Joshua Daryl Carrott, my master friend and root!"

"Hello, my old pal," said Josh with a broad grin.

"Hullo," said Ollie, like an idiot.

"I wasn't talking to you. Muncho's back in my imagination!"

"That's nice Josh," said Ollie, surreptitiously googling the word 'hallucinations'.

"Happy Birthday to You", sang Muncho happily. "Wanna win some money?"

And with that, the three of them swanned off together into the sunset.

ACKNOWLEDGEMENTS

I am hugely indebted to a multitude of people who have helped make this project possible. Firstly to Adam and Luke for reluctantly agreeing to let me do this again, knowing it makes no business sense whatsoever. To the whole JOLLY team, Grace Park, Aiden Lewis, Jordan Carrott, Josh Gibson, Rosemary Lim and Ducky Chang - I'm sorry that you have inevitably picked up some of the slack while I've toiled under the Sisyphean burden of my childish ambitions.

The writing process has been undertaken almost entirely by Jenny Lee and Andy Brierley, working off my wholly incomplete - and often incomprehensible - story outline. You are both funny, patient and generous, and I am enormously grateful for your friendships. Ben Thomas has once again illustrated a brilliant front cover, alongside twenty unique and evocative illustrations.

To everyone at Compass-Publishing UK, especially Alexa Whitten who guided me through the late-stage rigmarole of typesetting and publication.

To Dave Scott, Peggy Frew and the team from Carrotland in Ohakune, New Zealand - we love you! Hopefully we'll see you all again soon.

Lastly I wish to thank Ollie. What an amazing journey we've been on, buddy...

"I count myself in nothing else so happy, as in a soul remembering my good friends" – Richard II Act 2 Scene 2

Made in United States
Orlando, FL
20 December 2023

41483126R00071